Universal Design for Distance Education: A Guide for Online Course Development

Edited by
LaRon A. Scott
Colleen A. Thoma

XanEdu
Change the course.

Printed in the United States of America

ISBN 13: 978-1-50669-578-5

Cover Image: Designed by Jcomp - Freepik.com

XanEdu
Change the course.

530 Great Road
Acton, MA 01720
800-562-2147
www.xanedu.com

Contents

About the Authors

LaRon Scott, Ed.D., is an assistant professor and director of online programs in special education at Virginia Commonwealth University. He also coordinates the online M.Ed. program education, and is responsible for managing the improvement, recruitment, and support of online program candidates. He teaches graduate courses on clinical teaching, methods, collaboration, and universal design for learning. Dr. Scott has received funding from the Virginia Department of Education to support the development of online program and courses in special education. Dr. Scott completed the *Preparing to Teach Online* (PTTO) course through the Center for Teaching Excellence at VCU in 2012, bringing experience of effective online teaching strategies. He has authored books and manuscripts on improving teacher/personnel preparation programs and universal design for learning and transition planning for students with disabilities see *Universal Design for Transition: A Roadmap for Planning and Instruction.*

Colleen Thoma, PhD, is professor and chair of the Department of Counseling and Special Education in the School of Education at Virginia Commonwealth University. She is a nationally recognized leader in the area of self-determination and transition planning, particularly focusing on the preparation of teachers and related services personnel to facilitate self-determined transition planning for students with disabilities. She also conducts research on applications of a universal design for learning approach to transition planning, strategies to improve postschool outcomes for youth with disabilities, and the transition to postsecondary education. Dr. Thoma served as the president of the Division on Career Development and Transition of the Council for Exceptional Children, and currently is the president of the Education Division of the American Association on Intellectual and Developmental Disabilities. Dr. Thoma was a recent Ruderman Family Policy Fellow, working with the Collaboration to Promote Self-Determination (CPSD), was named a Fellow of the American Association on Intellectual and Developmental Disabilities (2014), received the Switzer Distinguished Research Fellowship from National Institute on Disability and Rehabilitation Research (NIDRR; 2012), and serves on the editorial boards of several special education journals.

About the Contributing Authors

K. Alisa Lowrey, PhD, is an associate professor, University of Southern Mississippi. Dr. Lowrey is a special educator with more than twenty-seven years of experience working with individuals with developmental disabilities, focusing specifically on individuals with intellectual disabilities and autism. Her research includes (a) teacher education, professional development, and evaluation, (b) inclusive educational practices including postsecondary practices for students with developmental disabilities, and the application of Universal Design for Learning, and (c) designing quality, individualized curricula. Dr. Lowrey currently serves as the co-editor of *Focus on Autism and Other Developmental Disabilities*. She also serves on the Universal Design for Learning Implementation and Research Network Leadership Board.

Kimberly Coy, PhD, is an assistant professor of education at California State University, Fresno. Before working in post secondary education, Dr. Coy taught K–8 general and special education, including working in a full time online public school. Kimberly has done extensive work—research, writing, and speaking—on UDL in a variety of educational environments. These include elementary, post secondary, and digital environments.

Monty Jones, PhD, is an assistant professor of instructional technology in the School of Education at Virginia Commonwealth University. Dr. Jones studies pre-service and in-service K–12 teacher learning of technology integration with a focus on technologies supporting online teaching and digital fabrication. He is the creator and program coordinator of the VCU Online Teaching Certificate Program, which prepares K–12 teachers to effectively teach in online and hybrid environments.

Christina Bartholomew, PhD, is an assistant professor in the Department of Counselor and Special Education at Virginia Commonwealth University. She serves as the Special Education Curriculum Director for the Richmond Teacher Residency Program, an urban teacher preparation program that integrates research-supported pedagogy with urban classroom experiences. Throughout her career, Dr. Bartholomew has focused on teacher preparation through her research and teaching. She has published, presented, and/or taught on topics such as universal design for learning, evidence-based instructional strategies, service learning in teacher preparation, effective literacy instruction, and the use of coaching strategies in professional development. She is also the co-author of the textbook *Universal Design for Transition: A Roadmap for Planning and Instruction.*

Jonathan Becker, PhD, is an associate professor of educational leadership at Virginia Commonwealth University, is the Director of Learning Innovation and Online Academic Programs in the Academic Learning Transformation Lab (ALT Lab) at VCU. After graduating from Duke University with a B.A. in public policy studies in 1994, Jonathan received a law degree and a masters degree from Boston College Law School and the Boston College Graduate School of Education in 1997. Additionally, in 2003, Jonathan earned a PhD in the politics of education from Teachers College, Columbia University. After serving for five years on the faculty of Hofstra University, Jonathan joined the faculty of Virginia Commonwealth University in 2007.

Laura Gogia, MD, PhD, is an independent educational researcher and designer specializing in mixed research methodologies, connected learning, and digital learning innovation. After completing a doctorate in educational research and evaluation at Virginia Commonwealth University (VCU), she served as a postdoctoral fellow at the VCU Academic Learning Transformation (ALT) Lab and research fellow for the American Association of School Librarians. Recent projects include developing innovative student assessment strategies, exploring the impact of data visualization and reporting on educational policy, and integrating digitally networked participatory culture into higher education, professional development, and adult learning environments.

Sean Smith, PhD, is a teacher, teacher educator, researcher, national presenter, and the parent of four school-age children, two having exceptionalities. With a background in the research and implementation of Universally Design for Learning (UDL) technology-based innovations for struggling learners and those with disabilities, Sean has authored books, chapters, articles, and offered hundreds of national presentations. The Principal Investigator (PI) or Co-PI on federally funded research and implementation projects, Sean is currently examining the impact of virtual reality and online learning on student development as well as ways to apply evidence-based technology innovations across the lives of those with exceptionalities, particularly in the area of literacy and technology.

A former coeditor of the *Journal of Special Education Technology* and *Teaching Exceptional Children*, Sean works to identify ways to further the research-to-practice gap to ensure effective and efficient outcomes for *all* learners, especially via innovative technology-based solutions.

Mary E. Morningstar, PhD, is an associate professor in the Department of Special Education at the University of Kansas and director of the Transition Coalition, which offers online, hybrid, and in-person professional development and resources for secondary special educators and transition practitioners. She coordinates the online transition master's program as well as the teacher education program for teachers of students with significant disabilities, working to transform special education coursework to support inclusive practices in schools and the community. Her research agenda includes evaluating the impact of secondary teacher quality and professional development on transition practices and student outcomes.

Monica Simonsen, PhD, is the director of Special Education Online Programs at the University of Kansas. In this capacity, she is responsible for ensuring the use of high quality online pedagogy across multiple programs, courses, and instructors. She is also the associate coordinator of the master's program in Secondary Special Education and Transition. Her primary research interests are the role of secondary school programing, transition services, and family expectations/engagement on the post-school outcomes of youth with disabilities.

Brianne L. Moore-Adams, a PhD candidate, is a virtual educator and curriculum designer for the Virtual Virginia Program in the School of Education at Virginia Commonwealth University. Her research focuses on teacher preparation for teaching online.

Peter Temple, a PhD candidate in special education and disability policy at Virginia Commonwealth University in Richmond, Virginia, has spent the last four years developing online coursework utilizing Universal Design for Learning as a framework for master's-level education. His research interest includes finding new solutions to innovative challenges in online learning.

Jobina Khoo, a PhD student in RESA: Research, Evaluations, Statistics, and Assessment, at The University of Southern Mississippi. She is employed as a graduate assistant in the Department of Curriculum, Instruction, and Special Education. In this capacity, she works as a production editorial assistant for Dr. Alisa Lowrey, co-editor of *Focus on Autism and Other Developmental Disabilities*.

Jingrong Xie, M.A., is a third year doctoral student in the special education department at University of Kansas. Her specialization is in Instructional Design, Technology, and Innovation (IDTI). Her research interest is in mobile learning, universal design for learning (UDL), and online education. She hopes to design and deliver products and services that are usable by people with the widest possible range of functional capabilities and to enhance the quality of life of persons with (dis)abilities and their families, especially to support women with disabilities in Science, Technology, Engineering, and Math (STEM) in post-secondary education.

Brittany Sterrett, M.Ed., is a second year doctoral student in special education and disability policy at Virginia Commonwealth University. She received her B.A. in political science with a concentration in legal studies from Virginia Tech and earned her M.Ed. in special education from Virginia Commonwealth University. She was a middle school special educator in the Richmond, VA area before enrolling in her doctoral program as one of three scholars representing Virginia Commonwealth University in the National Center for Leadership in Intensive Interventions consortium (led by Vanderbilt University). Her research interests include developing protocols for intensifying interventions for students at the middle school level with significant behavioral challenges.

Acknowledgements

We would like to acknowledge the amazing team of contributing authors that worked to bring the vision of this book to life. Your contributions are in part why this book is able to reach a wide-range of listeners interested in the possibilities of distance education. Thank you all for your responsiveness, your great suggestions and willingness to join us in this journey.

Next, we would like to thank our respective families. LaRon Scott thanks Dwight VanRossum and Morgan Scott, for their support during this process. It's the long nights of tolerating me working that makes you two my heroes. Thank you! Colleen Thoma thanks Michael and Chris Thoma who have always supported and encouraged her, and LaRon Scott, whose leadership in online learning is an inspiration.

Lastly, we would like to acknowledge the staff at XanEdu for their innovative design of this project. It only made sense for us to select this company after the multiple ways in which you are prepared to support the development, launch, and dissemination of this book. Our singular purpose for this book is to make distant learning and education accessible to all, and your company is prepared to help create that universal design for learning target that we aspire to achieve in this book.

LaRon and Colleen

1

Universal Design for Distance Education: A Framework for Delivering Online Courses

LaRon A. Scott
Colleen A. Thoma
VIRGINIA COMMONWEALTH UNIVERSITY

We remember the first discussion about the possibility of creating a fully online graduate-level teacher licensure program in our department. We already had an online certification-only option, but the thought of changing our full master's level program was seen as a radical departure. Faculty questioned whether one could adequately prepare a special educator if there were no opportunities to meet with them face-to-face, and to engage them in discussions designed to enhance their skills in critical reflection. This debate highlighted the need to educate faculty about online pedagogy, and introduce them to new technologies that could provide these kinds of experiences for online learners. We hope this book serves that purpose, extending that knowledge and skills to faculty beyond our department.

Introduction

Universal Design for Distance Education: A Framework for Delivering Online Courses was developed to introduce novice and seasoned professionals who wish to embark on distance education course and program design to a framework known as universal design for learning. One of the primary components of teaching and learning in distance education is the ability to create learning environments that are engaging, motivating, and provide access to contributors who share similar learning objectives (Salmon, 2002). Creating an online learning environment designed to consider the nuances of specialized content has the opportunity to positively influence preparation of students enrolled in distance education programs. Whereas more and more universities are choosing to convert traditional face-to-face programs to online programs (Newberry and Logofatu, 2008), there is little doubt that it is necessary for instructors to learn a new set of skills to engage learners by designing an online learning environment that effectively represents specialized learning topics. Standardized online course structures (e.g., navigational layout, arrangement of materials and information, communication tools) help reduce students' and faculty learning curve and increases efficiency of students' online learning experiences (Lee, Dickerson, and Winslow, 2012). With a specialized online course design, students' learning can be positively impacted (Scott, Temple, and Marshall, 2015).

This is where the idea of creating online courses designed to positively impact student learning in our program started. In researching and reviewing course designs for converting one of our graduate-level on-campus special education program to an online one, we determined that there was minimum support for faculty as they redesigned delivery methods and assessment of student progress. As a result, we designed an online course that we believe incorporated specialized curriculum, online pedagogy, and utilized the universal design for learning (UDL) guidelines that allowed all students to access learning based on their needs and interests. Our findings after we designed and delivered the course to a group of online graduate-level students revealed that the design and delivery yielded positive results towards their engagement and preparation during and after taking the course (Scott, Temple, and Marshall, 2015). This book was developed to help others who are in the process of developing their own online courses and/or programs. One of the main goals of this book is to highlight the model we developed for designing an online course and provide a roadmap for professionals seeking to design individual courses or who wish to build distance education programs.

Universal Design for Distance Education: A Guide for Online Course Development extends the literature on distance education; in particular the use of the Universal Design for Learning (UDL) framework in the online learning environment. The book includes ideas and design procedures from experts in the field of distance education and UDL. Experts help to bridge the gap in theory and application for building UDL into the design and delivery of online courses. This book is useful for faculty (e.g., deans, distance education administrators, professors, and staff) who are charged with research and development of distance education programs and online courses at the graduate and undergraduate levels. The proposed book can also serve as a guide for school districts in developing distance education courses. With the increase of online courses in PK–12 schools, who are increasingly addressing the needs of students from diverse learning backgrounds, having a framework for building effective online coursework is essential.

Each chapter focuses on distance education, and how universal design can be applied to a specific aspect of the design and delivery of distance education courses and programs. This book covers major topics of distance education and universal design for learning:

Section I provides an intricate overview of distance education and the UDL framework:

- Chapter two provides an introduction to distance education, including distance education models.
- Chapter three describes UDL, the framework for UDL, and the principles and guidelines for the framework.

Section II is arranged to explore each of the UDL guidelines and to identify specific strategies for their application in distance education:

- Chapter four explores the UDL principle of engagement and what tools, resources, and strategies are valued as ways this principle can be infused into distance education coursework.
- Chapter five describes the UDL principle of representation and what tools, resources, and strategies are valued as ways this principle can be infused into distance education coursework.
- Chapter six defines the UDL principle of expression and what tools, resources, and strategies are valued as ways this principle can be infused into distance education coursework.

Section III provides supports and examples for applying UDL to distance education models:

- Chapter seven provides thoughts on Web 2.0 tools and other applicable technology for distance education.
- Chapter eight illustrates an online course model or template that represents the desired UDL learning environment and wraps up the discussion about distance education and the UDL framework, providing final examples.

Universal Design for Distance Education: A Framework for Delivering Online Courses will help audiences improve the design and delivery of distance education coursework. We hope that this book will serve as a "how-to" for building effective distance education courses and programs.

2

Introduction to Distance Education

W. Monty Jones
Brianne Moore-Adams
VIRGINIA COMMONWEALTH UNIVERSITY

Distance education once referred to an asynchronous learning opportunity that relied on self-instruction. Students read material or listened to taped lectures and then completed assignments or tests designed to determine whether they acquired an understanding of key concepts. With the current explosion of technology and the ubiquitous nature of technology in life, our vision of what's possible in distance education needs to expand exponentially.

Introduction

The evolution of technology has transformed distance education, and modern virtual learning activities have little in common with the correspondence courses that were developed in the nineteenth century (Moore, 2005), or the subsequent first online courses at Open University in the United Kingdom in 1986 (Mason, 2000). However, from these early courses, distance education opportunities spread across Europe and into Canada, arriving in the United States in the early 1990s. By 2000, online learning had expanded from higher education to K12 environments. This growth has continued ever since (Kennedy and Archambault, 2012), with over 2,000,000 students enrolled in K12 online learning courses (Barbour and Unger, 2014) and over 5,500,000 students in higher education in the United States (National Center for Education Statistics, 2013).

The increasing growth of this field reflects the affordances of distance education in both higher education and K12 settings. Primarily, distance education can increase accessibility of learning opportunities for students.

Keeping Pace with K12 Digital Learning, an annual report on the status of Digital Learning across the United States, cites the origins of the earliest K12 online programs in rural America (Watson et al., 2015). In Canada as well, many early online programs began in rural areas where students lacked access to qualified teachers or needed courses (Barbour, 2007). Students in these situations are afforded learning opportunities through distance education that otherwise would not be possible due to their isolated geographic locations. Additionally, online learning allows students with special needs access to these educational alternatives. Students may choose distance education opportunities for a variety of reasons, such as extended illness, developmental or behavioral issues, scheduling conflicts due to participation in professional artistic or athletic endeavors, scheduling conflicts as a result of a lack of courses, or teacher shortages in specific content areas (Watson et al., 2015). Additionally, online learners gain valuable twenty-first century skills, such as the ability to learn independently as well as work collaboratively with classmates that may not be in close geographic proximity (Compton, 2009; Peters, 2005). Online learners also have the opportunity to enhance their media competencies (Peters, 2005) to keep up with the rapidly evolving technological landscape.

This chapter will examine the historical and conceptual foundations of distance education, identify current trends in this field, and look forward towards how emerging technologies may impact distance education in the future. These elements together illustrate the past, present, and future of distance education, and provide foundational knowledge in both theory and practice for readers interested in building effective online programs/courses utilizing the UDL framework.

Historical and Conceptual Foundations

One of the first educational theories to consider the unique context of learning at a distance was the Theory of Transactional Distance (Moore, 1993). This theory articulated the connections between three elements typical in distance education courses: structure, dialogue, and autonomy. Structure was considered in terms of the amount of agency learners held in regards to what was learned, how it was learned, and when it was learned. Dialogue referred the amount of interaction in which participants engaged. Transactional distance was described as a function of these two elements. For example, a course that was heavily structured in terms of learning activities, but offered little interaction between participants was viewed as having a high degree of transactional distance. This type of learning experience, Moore suggests, required a higher degree of learner autonomy.

Building upon Moore's framework, specifically in terms of structure and autonomy, Garrison, Anderson, and Archer (1999) developed the Community of Inquiry framework intended to "capture the educational dynamic and guide the study of online learning effectiveness in higher education" (Garrison and Akyol, 2013, p. 105). This framework proposes three elements of distance education environments that could contribute to higher-order thinking skills: social presence, cognitive presence, and teaching presence. Cognitive presence is defined by a learner's ability to think critically when presented with content in a computer-based setting (Garrison, Anderson, and Archer, 2010). Social presence is the learner's capability to present themselves in a virtual setting as a "real" person, both in social and emotional terms, while teaching presence is a synthesis of the design and the facilitation of the computer-based/distance experience. This theory, conceived from experiential analysis of theories of teaching and learning in higher education, was designed to serve as a starting point for educators to provide effective computer-based instruction (Garrison, Anderson, and Archer, 2010).

Finally, recognizing the impact of Web 2.0 tools such as blogs and social media in terms of increased interactivity over the Internet and its implications for knowledge acquisition, Siemens (2005) developed the Theory of Connectivism. Connectivism differs from other predominant learning theories in education such as behaviorism, cognitivism, and even constructivism, in that it was developed in response to technology impacting human interactions in a way that was both impossible and inconceivable when earlier learning theories were proposed (Siemens, 2005). Connectivism grounds itself in the idea that learning is achieved through a complex series of networks, created by the learner, who takes in the information, processes it and then transmits it back to the network using other forms of media (Kop, 2011). Connectivism represents a learning theory encompassing a visible shift in society, one where virtual interactions can lead to meaningful educational experiences.

Current Trends in Distance Education

To provide a brief illustration of the modern landscape of distance education we will examine current themes in both teaching and learning. We will examine the technological pedagogical content knowledge (Mishra and Koehler, 2006) conceptual framework for technology-rich teaching, and explore how this framework can be extended into distance education teaching practices. We will then describe the Massive Open Online Course model, which has garnered increased attention in the field in recent years. In considering distance education from the learners' perspectives, we will examine learner autonomy through the lens of self-regulated learning theory (Zimmerman 1990, 2001), and explore community development in distance education learning activities. The alignment of these themes with previously mentioned theoretical frameworks will be articulated to bring together theory and practice.

Teaching

Best practices for distance education teaching have traditionally been derived from best practices in face-to-face teaching. Teacher training for distance education has often occurred "on the job" and early research in the field of online teaching typically utilized autoethnographies and personal accounts of challenges faced in these new environments (Mason, 2000; Davis and Rose, 2007; DiPietro, Ferdig, Black, and Preston, 2008). While different challenges and opportunities exist in distance education contexts, there is value in extending what is known about technology-rich teaching in face-to-face contexts to distance education. For example, the technological pedagogical content knowledge framework (TPACK) (Mishra and Koehler, 2006) was derived as a modern extension of Shulman's Pedagogical Content Knowledge theory (1986), and suggests that effective technology-rich instruction is dependent on a teacher's specialized knowledge of the relationships between technology, pedagogy, and their specific content. This framework aligns well with the context of modern distance education environments in which technology is a ubiquitous element.

As research specific to teaching in distance education contexts has evolved, several studies have articulated best practices specific to this environment, and among these (DiPietro, et al., 2008; Compton, 2009; Davis and Rose, 2007; Ferdig, Cavanaugh, Black, and Dawson, 2009; Harms, Niederhauser, Davis, Roblyer, and Gilbert, 2006; Kennedy and Archambault, 2012; Rice and Dawley, 2009) nearly all align with the TPACK model in suggesting that instructors must effectively utilize the available technologies to facilitate understanding in a way that maximizes the affordances of the digital tools (DiPietro et al., 2008; Compton, 2009; Davis and Rose, 2007; Kennedy and Archambault, 2012; Rice and Dawley, 2009). Further, researchers suggest that virtual instructors must possess the ability to effectively communicate through digital tools (Rice and Dawley, 2009; DiPietro et al., 2008; Ferdig et al., 2009), as well as establish teacher presence (DiPietro et al., 2008; Harms et. al, 2006; Kennedy and Archambault, 2012). These practices, among many others listed in these studies, all correspond to different dimensions of the TPACK framework, giving teachers direction as to how they should proceed in this digital environment. While the TPACK framework provides initial guidance for considering effective teaching in distance education contexts, new distance education models, such as Massive Open Online Courses (MOOCS) will likely require additional research into teaching best practices in these settings.

The MOOC model was conceived at Stanford University in 2012 (Zemsky, 2014). In this model, courses are created, typically by large universities, and offered free of charge, to an unlimited number of participants. Enrollees can number in the tens of thousands and are often made up of an international student body. Often MOOCs utilize pre-recorded lecture-based videos, accompanied by downloadable notes. These materials are created in advance and grouped into modules that are released automatically without instructor intervention (MacDonald and Ahern, 2015). Assignments are often automatically graded, and may utilize peer-reviewed activities (Luo, Robinson, and Park, 2014). Various social networking techniques are employed and student-to-student communication in the form of discussion boards, forums, or social networking communities is encouraged (Chang, Hung, and Lin, 2015; Baggaley, 2013; Zemsky, 2014).

This method allows for increased public access to traditionally prohibitive learning opportunities in specialized fields (MacDonald and Ahern, 2015). Previously, access to fields of study such as artificial intelligence and other specialized content areas were limited to students pursuing degrees at institutions of higher education. Further, MOOCs may allow learners a greater degree of agency in terms of how and when they interact with the course (MacDonald and Ahern, 2015; Zemsky, 2014). Researchers, however, also suggest several constraints of MOOCs. For example, MOOCs may introduce an increased level of isolation for students, as inherent hurdles for the instructor to manually grade individual assignments or provide individual feedback (Luo, Robinson, and Park, 2014; Baggaley, 2013) may significantly reduce teacher-student interaction. Additionally, MOOCs have been shown to have greater attrition rates than other types of distance education opportunities (Zemsky, 2014; Baggaley, 2013; Chang,

Hung, and Lin, 2015). Students in MOOCs have reported several reasons for withdrawing from courses such as being overwhelmed by the number of peers in discussion forums and other interactions (Baggaley, 2013), problems with time management (Chang, Hung, and Lin, 2015), and lack of a final assessment or value measure (i.e., course credit) awarded at the end of the course (MacDonald and Ahern, 2015).

This original MOOC model, now referred to as the xMOOC, is based on instructionism (Chang, Hung, and Lin, 2015), and its primary focus is the attainment of specific course knowledge by the participants (Baggaley, 2013). In an attempt to differentiate from this model, researchers Siemens and Downes introduced the connectivist MOOC, or cMOOC model (Baggaley, 2013; Chang, Hung, and Lin, 2015). This model is often less structured, and promotes greater student interaction and exploration of the topic outside of the confines of the course content (Baggaley, 2013). In this model, knowledge is created by connecting learners within the social network of the MOOC (Baggaley, 2013; Chang, Hung, and Lin, 2015). In accordance with connectivist theory, the knowledge gained within this network is then disseminated to other nodes of information outside of the network.

Learning

To examine distance education from the lens of the learner, we will consider learners as both individuals and parts of a group. When considering students as individuals, we will focus on the increased agency that is afforded through distance education learning activities. In terms of individuals as part of a group, we will examine the concept of group development within distance education learning activities.

Geographically situating learners outside of the classroom is a fundamental premise of distance education, and the resultant increased level of student agency may necessitate an increased level of self-regulation in terms of student learning processes. This perspective was put forth in Moore's (1993) theory of transactional distance where it is suggested that as distance learning opportunities increased in transactional distance, greater learner autonomy would be required by students to be successful. Researchers in the field of educational psychology have further developed this idea of learner autonomy, and defined the construct of self-regulated learning (SRL) as "the self-directive process through which learners transform their mental abilities into task related academic skills" (Zimmerman, 2001, p. 1). However, SRL is not solely concerned with asocial forms of learning, but also social strategies such as feedback from peers, teachers, or coaches (Zimmerman, 2001). A common way to characterize SRL is through metacognition, motivation, and behavior (Zimmerman, 1990). Metacognitive learning processes include planning, setting goals, organizing, self-monitoring, and self-evaluation. Motivation and learning are viewed within this framework as interdependent processes, and motivation to learn goes beyond executing a learning response, but instead involves a learner's proactive efforts to "seek out and profit from learning activities" (Zimmerman, 1990, p. 6).

Several studies have noted that within virtual learning environments, students may be less effective without the ability to regulate their learning (Azevedo, Fielding, and Moos, 2004; Lynch and Dembo, 2004; Puzziferro, 2008). However, SRL is not entirely dependent on the individual but can also be a function of their learning environment (Dettori and Persico, 2008), and several studies have suggested that student SRL can be improved through the use of distance education learning activities (Lewis and Litchfield, 2011). Research into the role of the learning environment to facilitate SRL provides several insights for improving the structure of distance education learning environments (see Baggetun and Wasson, 2006; Barber, Bagsby, Grawitch, and Buerck, 2011; Lenne, Abel, and Trigano, 2008; Trigano, 2006). Researchers have examined the use of social media components such as cyber "pokes" within Facebook (Bowers-Campbell, 2008), the use of online help within a distance education course (Cheng, Liang, and Tsai, 2013), and how collaborative aspects of online learning experiences can help foster the SRL abilities in students (Dettori, Giannetti, and Persico, 2006).

The relationship between SRL and distance education is complex in that distance education learning activities may both require a certain level of SRL by the students to be successful, and also help develop SRL proficiencies (Dettori and Persico, 2008). Effectively designed distance education learning activities can prompt students to reflect on their learning, assist students in proactively planning, and provide channels for help-seeking. However, several studies have also positively correlated existing student SRL skills with higher performance in distance education learning activities (Joo, Bong, and Choi, 2000).

One of the most promising lines of research concerning these two areas examines the effects of providing SRL training to participants in distance education courses. Several studies have suggested that this type of training is positively correlated with improved course performance

(Hu and Driscoll, 2013; Santhanam and Sasidharan, 2008). This line of research also indicates that simply moving teaching materials into a distance education format may not be effective without providing additional instruction on SRL strategies (Shen, Lee, and Tsai, 2008). Future research in this area, bridging both educational psychology and educational technology, may help to uncover fundamental hurdles learners experience in distance education learning activities, and provide strategies to overcome these hurdles. Findings from these studies may assist a wider population of students in becoming successful in distance education initiatives, and continue to advance research in this field.

In consideration of the individual as part of a larger group, social isolation and lack of community has often been a criticism of distance education (Mason, 2000; Peters, 2005). Learners may feel isolated from their instructors and peers or even detached from the learning process itself (Boulos, Taylor, and Breton, 2005; Fleckenstein, 2005; Black, Dawson, and Priem, 2008). Often it is reported that virtual learning environments lack social cues such as such as body language and eye contact (Boulos, Taylor, and Breton, 2005). However, there has been an increasing interest in overcoming these hurdles through improving online community in virtual environments and understanding how this may affect online learners (Shea, 2006). The Community of Inquiry framework (Garrison, Anderson, and Archer, 1999) provides some guidance to partially address this concern. Teacher presence, an important element of the online community, has been linked to student success as students that perceive themselves as part of a community have been shown to have greater overall academic achievement and motivation (Kiefer, Allerbrock, and Alley, 2014). A study by Black, Dawson, and Priem (2008) found that students who felt as if they were a part of an online learning community and felt connected to other community members, were more likely to log into their virtual course more frequently than those students that did not feel as strong a connection. These connections contribute to lower attrition rates (Shea, 2006) and more supportive learning communities (Fleckenstein, 2005).

Another way by which online educators can facilitate a sense of community in online courses is by using synchronous learning activities. The expansion of web-based synchronous communication tools as well as increased access to high-speed internet have made synchronous communication sessions increasingly accessible (Aras et al., 2015). Synchronous communication allows for students and teachers to interact with one another in real-time through text, voice, and video. Mathematics and science teachers also have an array of applications available to them that allow them to demonstrate in real-time complex calculations and labs, and answer student questions when they arise (Barbour and Unger, 2014).

Future Directions

The evolution of digital communication technologies advanced the field of distance education from mail correspondence courses to rich interactive virtual environments that facilitate robust communication among students and teachers, and allows students to interact with global virtual resources. Emerging technologies are continuing this evolution as the environments in which distance education learning activities are conducted are becoming more complex, more interactive, and provide features not possible in non-digital environments.

Second Life (Linden Research, 2016) is a three dimensional virtual environment, where users can create avatars of themselves and interact with other users in a virtual world. This environment promotes active participation, and can provide students situations where answers must be sought out and problems explored as is done in many video game scenarios (Ferguson, 2011). In Second Life, participants may also create virtual buildings that simulate face-to-face classrooms to mimic the classroom experience (Warburton, 2009; Ferguson, 2011), promoting a greater sense of community than may be provided in a typical LMS (Warburton, 2009).

Minecraft (TeacherGaming LLC, 2015) is a virtual environment geared toward younger participants, and uses a less realistic pixelated cartoon-block world that users can manipulate themselves, from the creation of their own characters to building elaborate cities and towns. Minecraft can be used for a variety of educational applications, such as teaching students the concepts of ecology and biology, applying mathematical measurement and applied problem solving (Short, 2012), developing architectural designs (Tromba, 2013), and creating digital art (Overby and Jones, 2015). Advocates for utilizing Minecraft in education cite enhanced student engagement and self-regulated learning, as students actively seek to solve teacher-manipulated problems presented within the virtual world (Tromba, 2013; Overby and Jones, 2015). Like Second Life, students working in the Minecraft environment can create avatars that navigate the environment, as well as construct virtual classrooms, schools, habitats, ecosystems, even entire cities and towns (TeacherGaming LLC, 2015).

Historically, the field of distance education sought to replicate the experience of classroom learning over greater geographical distances.

However, with advancements in digital communication technologies, the field now looks to improve on traditional face-to-face teaching methods. Emerging technologies such as virtual worlds provide students with the ability to build vast virtual structures, to redesign themselves as they envision in their imagination, and to collaborate with others across the globe. Students have the ability to ask question anonymously and to seek out support from others with similar interests. These technologies have the ability to minimize students' physical limitations and incentivize greater participation in learning activities. As the field of distance education progresses, we envision the benefits uncovered by these technologies not only improving education at a distance but improving education in all contexts.

References

Azevedo, R., Winters, F. I., and Moos, D. C. (2004). "Can students collaboratively use hypermedia to learn science? The dynamics of self- and other-regulatory processes in an ecology classroom." *Journal of Educational Computing Research*, 31(3), 215–245.

Baggaley, J. (2013). "MOOC rampant." *Distance Education*, 34(3), 368–378.

Baggetun, Rune, and Wasson, Barbara. (2006). "Self-regulated learning and open writing." *European Journal of Education*, 41(4), 453–472.

Barber, L., Bagsby, P., Grawitch, M., and Buerck, J. (2011). "Facilitating self-regulated learning with technology." *Teaching of Psychology*, 38(4), 303–308.

Barbour, M. K. (2007). "Principles of effective web-based content for secondary school students: Teacher and developer perceptions." *International Journal of E-Learning & Distance Education*, 21(3), 93–114.

Barbour, M. K., and Unger, K. L. (2014). "Strategies for overcoming common obstacles in the online environment: Issues in virtual school teaching." In A. A. Piña and A. P. Mizell (Eds.) *Real Life Distance Education: Case Studies in Practice* (pp. 21–40). Charlotte, NC: Information Age Publishing.

Black, E. W., Dawson, K., and Priem, J. (2008). "Data for free: Using LMS activity logs to measure community in online courses." *The Internet and Higher Education*, 11(2), 65–70.

Boulos, M., Taylor, A., and Breton, A. (2005). "A synchronous communication experiment within an online distance learning program: A case study." *Telemedicine Journal and E-health: The Official Journal of the American Telemedicine Association,* 11(5), 583–93.

Bowers-Campbell, J. (2008). "Cyber 'pokes': Motivational antidote for developmental college readers." *Journal of College Reading and Learning,* 39(1), 74–87.

Bozkurt, A., Akgun-Ozbek, E., Yilmazel, S., Erdogdu, E., Ucar, H., Guler, E., . . . Aydin, C. H. (2015). "Trends in distance education research: A content analysis of journals 2009–2013." *International Review of Research in Open and Distance Learning*, 16(1).

Chang, R. I., Hung, Y. H., and Lin, C. F. (2015). "Survey of learning experiences and influence of learning style preferences on user intentions regarding MOOCs." *British Journal of Educational Technology*, 46(3), 528–541.

Cheng, K. H., Liang, J. C., and Tsai, C. C. (2013). "University students' online academic help seeking: The role of self-regulation and information commitments." *The Internet and Higher Education*, 16, 70–77.

Compton, L. K. (2009). "Preparing language teachers to teach language online: A look at skills, roles, and responsibilities." *Computer Assisted Language Learning*, 22(1), 73–99.

Davis, N., and Rose, R. (2007). "Research committee issues brief: Professional development for virtual schooling and online learning." *North American Council for Online Learning*.

Dettori, G., Giannetti, T., and Persico, D. (2006). "SRL in online cooperative learning: Implications for pre-service teacher training." *European Journal of Education*, 41(3–4), 397–414.

Dettori, G., and Persico, D. (2008). "Detecting self-regulated learning in online communities by means of interaction analysis." *IEEE Transactions on Learning Technologies*, 1(1), 11–19.

DiPietro, M., Ferdig, R. E., Black, E. W., and Preston, M. (2008). "Best practices in teaching K–12 online: lessons learned from Michigan Virtual school teachers." *Journal of Interactive Online Learning*, 7(1), 10–35.

Ferdig, R. E., Cavanaugh, C., DiPietro, M., Black, E. W., and Dawson, K. (2009). "Virtual schooling standards and best practices for teacher education." *Journal of Technology and Teacher Education*, 17(4), 479–503.

Ferguson, Rebecca. (2011). "Meaningful learning and creativity in virtual worlds." *Thinking Skills and Creativity*, 6(3), 169–178.

Fleckenstein, K. (2005). "Faceless students, virtual places: Emergence and communal accountability in online classrooms." *Computers and Composition*, 22(2), 149–176.

Garrison, D. R., and Akyol, Z. (2013). "The community of inquiry theoretical framework." *Handbook of Distance Education*, 3, 104–120.

Garrison, D. R., Anderson, T., and Archer, W. (1999). "Critical inquiry in a text-based environment: Computer conferencing in higher education." *The Internet and Higher Education*, 2(2), 87–105.

Garrison, D. R., Anderson, T., and Archer, W. (2010). "The first decade of the community of inquiry framework: A retrospective." *The Internet and Higher Education*, 13(1), 5–9.

Harms, C. M., Niederhauser, D. S., Davis, N. E., Roblyer, M. D., and Gilbert, S. B. (2006). "Educating educators for virtual schooling: Communicating roles and responsibilities." *Electronic Journal of Communication*, 16(1–2), 17–24.

Hu, H., and Driscoll, M. (2013). "Self-regulation in e-learning environments: A remedy for community college?" *Journal of Educational Technology & Society*, 16(4).

Joo, Y., Bong, M., and Choi, H. (2000). "Self-efficacy for self-regulated learning, academic self-efficacy, and internet self-efficacy in Web-based instruction." *Educational Technology Research and Development*, 48(2), 5–17.

Kennedy, K., and Archambault, L. (2012). "Offering preservice teachers field experiences in k–12 online learning: A national survey of teacher education programs." *Journal of Teacher Education*, 63(3), 185–200.

Kiefer, S. M., Ellerbrock, C., and Alley, K. (2014). "The role of responsive teacher practices in supporting academic motivation at the middle level." *RMLE Online*, 38(1), 1–16.

Kop, R. (2011). "The challenges to connectivist learning on open online networks: Learning experiences during a massive open online course." *The International Review of Research in Open and Distributed Learning*, 12(3), 19–38.

Lenne, D., Abel, M. H., Trigano, P., and Leblanc, A. (2008). "Self-regulated learning in Technology Enhanced Learning Environments: An investigation with university students." *Technology, Pedagogy and Education*, 17(3), 171–181.

Lewis, J. P. and Litchfield, B. C. (2011). "Effects of self-regulated learning strategies on preservice teachers in an educational technology course." *Education*, 132 (2), 455–464.

Linden Research, Inc. (2016). "What is Second Life?" Retrieved from http://secondlife.com/whatis/.

Luo, H., Robinson, A. C., and Park, J. Y. (2014). "Peer grading in a MOOC: Reliability, validity, and perceived effects." *Journal of Asynchronous Learning Networks*, 18(2).

Lynch, R., and Dembo, M. (2004). "The relationship between self-regulation and online learning in a blended learning context." *The International Review of Research in Open and Distributed Learning*, 5(2).

MacDonald, P., and Ahern, T. C. (2015). "Exploring the instructional value and worth of a MOOC." *Journal of Educational Computing Research*. 52(4), 496–513.

Mason, R. (2000). "From distance education to online education." *The Internet and higher education*, 3(1), 63–74.

Mishra, P., and Koehler, M. (2006). "Technological pedagogical content knowledge: A framework for teacher knowledge." *The Teachers College Record*, 108(6), 1017–1054.

TeacherGaming LLC. (2015). "What is MinecraftEdu?" Retrieved from http://minecraftedu.com/about.

Moore, M. G. (1993). "Theory of transactional distance." *Theoretical principles of distance education*, 22.

Moore, M. G. (Ed.). (2005). *Handbook of distance education*. New York, NY: Routledge.

National Center for Education Statistics. (2013). *Fast Facts: Distance Learning*. Retrieved from https://nces.ed.gov/fastfacts/display.asp?id=80.

Overby, Alexandra, and Jones, Brian L. (2015). "Virtual LEGOs: Incorporating Minecraft into the art education curriculum." *Art Education*, 68(1), 21–27.

Puzziferro, Maria. (2008). "Online technologies self-efficacy and self-regulated learning as predictors of final grade and satisfaction in college-level online courses." *American Journal of Distance Education*, 22(2), 72–89.

Peters, O. (2005). "Learning with new media in distance education." In Moore, M. G. and Anderson, W. G. (Eds.), *Handbook of Distance Education*. (pp. 87–112). Mahwah, NJ: Lawrence Erlbaum Associates, Inc.

Rice, K., and Dawley, L. (2009). "The status of professional development for K–12 online teachers: Insights and implications." *Journal of Technology and Teacher Education*, 17(4), 523–545.

Santhanam, R., Sasidharan, S., and Webster, J. (2008). "Using self-regulatory learning to enhance e-learning-based information technology training." *Information Systems Research*, 19(1), 26–47.

Shea, P. (2006). "A study of students' sense of learning community if online environments." *Journal of Asynchronous Learning Networks*, 10(1). 35–44.

Shen, P. D., Lee, T. H., and Tsai, C. W. (2008). "Enhancing skills of application software via web-enabled problem-based learning and self-regulated learning: An exploratory study." *Journal of Distance Education Technologies*, 6(3), 69–84.

Short, Daniel. (2012). "Teaching scientific concepts using a virtual world-Minecraft." *Teaching Science*, 58(3), 55–58.

Siemens, G. (2005). "Connectivism: A learning theory for the digital age." *International Journal of Instructional Technology & Distance Learning*, 2(1). Retrieved from http://www.itdl.org/Journal/Jan_05/article01.htm.

Shulman, L. S. (1986). "Those who understand: Knowledge growth in teaching." *Educational Researcher*, 15(2), 4–14.

Trigano, P. (2006). "Self-Regulated Learning in a TELE at the Université de Technologie de Compiègne: an analysis from multiple perspectives." *European Journal of Education*, 41(3-4), 381–395.

Tromba, Peter. (2013). "Build engagement and knowledge one block at a time with Minecraft." *Learning & Leading with Technology*, 40(8), 20–23.

Warburton, S. (2009). "Second Life in higher education: Assessing the potential for and the barriers to deploying virtual worlds in learning and teaching." *British Journal of Educational Technology*, 40(3), 414–426.

Watson, J., Pape, L., Gemin, B., and Vashaw, L. (2015). "Keeping pace with K–12 digital learning: An annual review of policy and practice." *Evergreen Education Group*.

Zemsky, R. (2014). "With a MOOC MOOC here and a MOOC MOOC there, here a MOOC, there a MOOC, everywhere a MOOC MOOC." *The Journal of General Education*, 63(4), 237–243.

Zimmerman, B. J. (1990). "Self-regulated learning and academic achievement: An overview." *Educational Psychologist*, 25(1), 3–17.

Zimmerman, B. J. (2001) "Theories of self-regulated learning and academic achievement: An overview and analysis." In Zimmerman, B. J. and Schunk, D. H. (Eds.), *Self-Regulated Learning and Academic Achievement: Theoretical Perspectives*, pp. 1–65. Mahwah, NJ: Lawrence Erlbaum Associates.

3

Introduction to Universal Design for Learning

Christina Bartholomew
Brittany Irving
VIRGINIA COMMONWEALTH UNIVERSITY

We first learned about Universal Design for Learning (UDL) in our teacher preparation master's level program. As teachers, we applied the UDL framework in our K–12 classrooms and soon began to see the positive impact UDL had on the children we served. Incorporating the UDL educational framework in order to include all learners was sensible, even in our work in higher education. With the opportunity to reach more learners using distance education practices, we believe the UDL blueprint is crucial for instructors seeking to meet the needs of diverse groups of students in higher education.

Universal Design For Learning

The concept of Universal Design for Learning (UDL) continues to grow in popularity as the research of its effectiveness in supporting the learning of diverse student populations continues to expand. A simple definition of UDL establishes it as a research based framework in which teaching and learning can be optimized for all people (CAST, 2016). This framework provides a set of three principles for creating instructional goals, methods, materials, and assessments that work for everyone. The principles of UDL are based in the neuroscience research about how individuals learn, engage in, and retain the information being taught, and are designed to proactively break down barriers to learning by providing multiple means of representation, engagement, and expression in learning opportunities (UDL Center, 2016). By applying these principles to their teaching practices, educators can flexibly plan for the diverse needs in the classroom. This chapter will explore the principles and guidelines of UDL, highlight some of the research behind this innovative concept, and explore how UDL can be effective across different curricula.

Theoretical Background behind UDL

The guiding principles of UDL were created through the fusion of multiple domains of education and cognitive research. Prominent psychologist Lev Vgotsky (1978, 1986) argued three conditions must be met for learning to take place: learning requires recognition of patterns acquired through sensory data collection, having access to strategies to respond to the perceived patterns, and engagement with both the sensory data and response strategies (Pisha and Coyne, 2001). Modern cognitive neuroimaging also reveals three broad divisions of learning within the brain that correspond with Vgotsky's optimal learning conditions: pattern recognition competencies in the posterior of the cortex, motor and executive competencies in the front of the cortex, and the emotional capabilities housed in the nervous system (Rose and Gravel, 2010; Pisha and Coyne, 2001). UDL builds upon these findings and identifies three corresponding neurological networks: the recognition network, the strategic network, and the affective network.

There is systematic variability across all learners in how these systems function in the learning process, and impacts what individuals learn, how they learn, and why they learn. Research supporting UDL suggests that there is no such thing as a "typical learner" (UDL center, 2016). If practitioners are to be effective in teaching all students, they should address this variability through their instructional resources, activities, and methods. The three guiding UDL principles, multiple means of representation, expression, and engagement, provide the foundation of this framework and establish guidelines for practitioners to consider when planning how to meet the variety of learners in their classroom. **Table 3.1** represents the connections among the neurological networks and the guiding principles of UDL.

Table 3.1: Neurological Networks and Guiding Principles of UDL

Network	Description	Guiding Principle
Recognition	Fact gathering Categorizing what is seen, heard, and read	Multiple Means of Representation
Strategic	Organizing ideas Expressing ideas	Multiple Means of Expression
Affective	Connecting the learning experience to an emotional background Determining engagement and motivation	Multiple Means of Engagement

Adapted from "UDL in Online College Coursework: Insights of Infusion and Educator Preparedness," by L. A. Scott, P. Temple, and D. Marshall, 2015, Online Learning, *19, p. 101.*

Multiple Means of Representation

The guiding principle of multiple means of representation seeks to reduce barriers associated with acquiring sensory data from the recognition system. During the learning process, individuals perceive and categorize information in a variety of ways. In addition, individuals enter the learning process with different learning strategies, abilities, and experiences, all of which impact them as a learner. To be effective and proactive in removing obstacles to learning, multiple opportunities should be provided for students to see, hear, read, and manipulate information. Information should also be thoughtfully displayed and communicated to learners, and UDL suggests that a variety of methods be used to present information while providing a range of supports that help individuals to access the information (CAST, 2016).

As seen in Table 3.1, this principle of UDL supports what is understood about the recognition network of the brain. This networks identifies and processes the five senses and enable individuals to understand information and concepts. Consequently, students will process materials with varied associations and at varied cognitive levels. Under the principles of UDL, practitioners should represent information by using numerous strategies that engage individuals through use of their multiple senses. Studies suggest practitioners who combine the use of visual diagrams and auditory explanations instruct inexperienced learners more effectively (Kalyuga, Chandler, and Sweller, 2000). Empirical research also shows illustrations are an effective supplement to text (Carney and Levin, 2002), and can support individual reading at different levels. By planning proactively to represent the information being taught in a multi-encompassing format, practitioners decrease the chances of not meeting the diverse needs and learning abilities of their students.

The UDL framework outlines three supporting guidelines to help direct practitioners in implementing the principle of Multiple Means of Representation in their practice. These guidelines include: provide multiple options for perception, provide multiple options for language and symbols, and provide multiple options for comprehension. (UDL center, 2016). **Table 3.2** provides several examples of classroom experiences and course materials utilizing the above guidelines.

Table 3.2: Multiple Means of Representation Guidelines

Options for Perception	Options for Language and Symbols	Options for Comprehension
Use of large fonts with text displays projected on the screen and other learning materials. Provide multiple visual and auditory modalities. Provide captions for videos. Use manipulatives and hands on learning activities.	Preteach important vocabulary and symbols. Incorporate visual supports to clarify vocabulary (i.e., pictures and videos). Make connections to previously learned materials. Break complex concepts into smaller, more easily understood parts.	Activate background knowledge through discussions or with the use of advanced organizers (i.e., KWL charts). Scaffold instruction with explicit prompts for each concept or step in process. Make cross-curricular connections. Provide options for organizing material and note taking.

Adapted from Center for Applied Special Technology, 2011

Multiple Means of Expression

Research of The Strategic Networks of the brain shows that individuals monitor, plan, and strategize in almost all aspects of life (CAST, 2016). Prioritizing and planning strategies and abilities vary across individuals and can impact the way individuals approach different tasks throughout the learning process. By understanding this need, practitioners can scaffold supports into instruction so that all students can express their knowledge of the content and fully engage in the learning process.

Students also enter the classroom with different background knowledge and experiences. Research shows that the stimulation of students' prior knowledge enhances comprehension because it promotes distinctive connections to the material (Spires and Donley, 1998). As individuals process new information they connect it with what they have seen, learned, and previously experienced. These connections promote higher level thinking (Spires and Donley, 1998). UDL also suggests that if practitioners are to engage all students in their classroom, they must be willing to provide several different types of activities for students to express their knowledge and questions. In addition, they must allow students to build upon their varied experiences so that they can effectively process and explore the content at diverse cognitive levels.

Benjamin Bloom, and his work with a hierarchical continuum of learning goals and objectives also influenced the guiding principle of multiple means of expression (Rose and Gravel, 2010). Bloom's Taxonomy breaks learning into six categories: knowledge, comprehension, application, analysis, synthesis, and evaluation. These categories identify a varied level of engagement and knowledge acquisition and move from simple to complex and from concrete to abstract (Krathrohl, 2002). Students will meet targeted learning objectives at different levels and in different ways. The guiding UDL principle of multiple means of expression suggests that teachers extend this thinking to include multiple options for expressing knowledge and ideas. Three guidelines are established in the UDL framework to support practitioners as they implement this principle in their curriculum development and instruction; these include: provide options for physical action, provide options for expressive skills and fluency, and provide options for executive functions (UDL center, 2016). **Table 3.3** provides examples of instructional opportunities for these guidelines.

Table 3.3: Multiple Means of Expression and Action Guidelines

Options for Physical Movement	Options for Expressive Skills and Fluency	Options for Executive Functions
Provide alternatives to writing by hand by allowing students to use a word processor or orally dictate their responses. Incorporate the use of assistive technology into assignments.	Allow students to use a variety of strategies to respond to or solve problems. Provide options for spelling and grammar checkers, word prediction software. Allow students to express their answers with the use of pictures.	Set and display classroom goals. Provide checklists and project templates to allow for scaffolding and student progress monitoring. Model different strategies to successfully complete assignments.

Adapted from Center for Applied Special Technology, 2011

Multiple Means of Engagement

Student motivation is an important factor in the learning process, and students' attitudes towards content and learning activities vary significantly. In addition, as students gain more knowledge and are exposed to more learning opportunities, their motivations and interests change. Addressing these changes can be a struggle for practitioners as they plan activities in their classroom. If students are not motivated to learn or are not engaged in the content or activities planned, the learning objectives become inaccessible. As mentioned earlier in the chapter, students enter the learning process with varied backgrounds and experiences. As a practitioner one must consider how to motivate students to build upon these unique entry points and actively engage all students in the new content. UDL has been shown to increase student engagement during instruction (Marino, Gotch, Israel, Vasquez, Basham, and Becht, 2014). On task behavior and higher student satisfaction have also been reported in classrooms using the UDL framework (Kortering, McClannon, and Braziel, 2008). The multiple means of engagement principle of UDL provides a framework to address student variability in engagement and motivation so that they are able to meet the learning objectives and goals (CAST, 2016). Three UDL guidelines are established to support this principle: options for recruiting interest, options for sustaining efforts and persistence, and options for self-regulation. **Table 3.4** outlines the guidelines used to support practitioners in considering how to motivate and engage students who demonstrate variability in their interests and attitudes.

Table 3.4: Multiple Means of Expression Guidelines

Options for Recruiting Interest	Options for Sustaining Effort and Persistence	Options for Self-Regulation
Promote autonomy by allowing as much student discretion as possible. Allow students to contribute to the creation of activities and assignments. Vary instruction so that it is responsive to student interests, preferences, and needs. Foster an accepting and supportive classroom environment. Provide a variety of sensory stimulations.	Engage learners in goal setting and monitoring with scaffolding. Emphasize student effort and the process of learning with achieving goals. Vary difficulty levels within activities. Create cooperative learning groups with explicit expectations, goals, roles, and responsibilities. Provide frequent and specific feedback to students.	Provide modeling, visuals, organizers, and checklists that encourage appropriate goal setting and achievement based on students' strengths and weaknesses. Provide varying materials for students to chart their own behaviors to promote self-regulation. Provide modeling and support for displaying appropriate coping skills needed for various situations.

Adapted from Center for Applied Special Technology, 2011.

Application of UDL

UDL is designed to create environments that anticipate the needs of diverse learners (Rose and Gravel, 2010). The framework's commitment to flexibility promotes its use across various age groups, disciplines, and levels of cognitive functioning. UDL's expanded use has influenced post secondary education, online learning, and the overall culture of classrooms.

Although typically considered for implementation by K–12 educators, UDL is increasingly being used in postsecondary education to provide a conceptual framework that makes teaching and adult learning more inclusive. In addition, equitable learning opportunities are being created with the use of accessible instruction and course materials. The acceptance of this framework by colleges and universities not only provides a solid foundation of evidence-based practices that benefits all students, but is responsive to the needs of the growing numbers of students with disabilities pursuing a college degree (Davies, Schelly, and Spooner, 2013).

Recent scholarship has also focused on UDL' s use in distance and online learning (Parker, Robinson, and Hannafin, 2008). Numerous post-secondary schools are moving away from the traditional face-to-face classroom instruction in favor of online courses. These schools see online learning experiences as opportunities to expand students' access to secondary education; however, barriers for student learning still exist with this type of instruction, especially for students with disabilities (Dell, Dell, and Blackwell, 2015). The UDL framework can be particularly useful in developing online coursework because of its commitment to infusing technology into instruction while accommodating the needs of all learners. UDL based online courses show promise with providing multiple representations of learning materials, authentic and self-directed learning activities, and opportunities to reflect within a community of learners (Scott, Temple, and Marshall, 2015; Parker, Robinson, and Hannafin, 2008). Overall, UDL has the potential to further the inclusion movement by addressing students' learning needs within various environments. It also has the potential to increase culturally informed learning experiences to help develop competencies needed for success in the twenty-first century. (Chita-Tegmark, Gravel, Serpa, Domings, and Rose 2012).

Conclusion

UDL establishes a guiding framework that can be flexibly used across disciplines to increase learning, engagement, and expressive opportunities for all learners. Grounded in neuroscience research, UDL establishes itself as a model consisting of evidence-based practices designed to reduce existing barriers to learning. By incorporating UDL into instruction and classroom environments, educators create multiple pathways for student success.

References

Abell, M. M., Jung, E., and Taylor, M. (2011). "Students' perceptions of classroom instructional environments in the context of universal design for learning." *Learning Environments Research*, 14, 171–185. doi: 10.1007/s10984-011-90902.

Carney, R. N. and Levin, J. R. (2002). "Pictorial illustrations still improve students' learning from text." *Educational Psychology Review*, 14(1), 5–26.

CAST (2011). *Universal Design for Learning Guidelines*, version 2.0. Wakefield, MA: Author.

Chita-Tegmark, M., Gravel, J. W., Serpa, M. B., Domings, Y., and Rose, D. H. (2012). "Using the universal design for learning framework to support culturally diverse learners." *Journal of Education*, 192(1), 17–22.

Davies, P. L., Schelly, C. L., and Spooner, C. L. (2013). "Measuring the effectiveness of universal design for learning intervention in postsecondary education." *Journal of Postsecondary Education and Disability*, 26(3), 195–220.

Dell, C. A., Dell, T. F., and Blackwell, T. L. (2015). "Applying universal design for learning in online courses: Pedagogical and practical considerations." *Journal of Educators Online*, 12(2). 166–192.

Kalyuga, S., Chandler, P., and Sweller, J. (2000). "Incorporating learner experience into the design of multimedia instruction." *Journal of Educational Psychology*, 92(1), 126–136.

Kortering, L. J., McClannon, T. W., and Braziel, P. M. (2008). "Universal design for learning: A look at what algebra and biology students with and without high incidence conditions are saying." *Remedial and Special Education*, 29, 352–363 doi: 10.1177/0741932507314020.

Krathwohl, D. R. (2002). "A revision of bloom's taxonomy: An overview." *Theory Into Practice*, 41(4), 212–218.

Parker, D. R., Robinson, L. E., and Hannafin, R. D. (2008). "Blending" technology and effective pedagogy in a core course for preservice teachers." *Journal of Computing in Teacher Education*, 24, 49–54.

Pisha, B., and Coyne P. (2001). "Smart from the start." *Remedial and Special Education*, 22(4), 197–__.

Marino, M. T., Gotch, C., Israel, M., Vasquez, E. III, Basham, J. D., and Becht, K. (2014). "UDL in the middle school science classroom: Can video games and alternative text heighten engagement and learning for students with learning disabilities?" *Learning Disability Quarterly*, 37, 87–99.

Rose, D. H. and Gravel, J. W. (2010). "Universal design for learning." In E. Baker, P. Peterson, and B. McGaw (Eds.) *International Encyclopedia of Education*, 3rd Ed. Oxford: Elsevier.

Scott, L. A., Temple, P., and Marshall, D. (2015). "UDL in online college coursework: Insights of infusion and educator preparedness." *Online Learning*, 19(5), 99–119.

Seufert, T. (2003). "Supporting coherence formation in learning from multiple representations." *Learning and Instruction*, 13(2), 227–237. doi:10.1016/S09594752(02)00022-1.

Spires, H. A., and Donley, J. (1998). "Prior knowledge activation: Inducing engagement with informational texts." *Journal of Educational Psychology*, 90(2), 249. http://dx.doi.org/10.1037/0022 0663.90.2.249.

Vgotsky, L. S. (1978). *Mind in Society: the Development of Higher Psychological Processes*. Cambridge, MA: Harvard University Press.

Vgotsky, L. S. (1986). *Thought and Language* (A. Kozulin, Trans.) Cambridge, MA: MIT Press.

4

Multiple Means of Representation In Distance Education

K. Alisa Lowrey, PhD

UNIVERSITY OF SOUTHERN MISSISSIPPI

Sean J. Smith, PhD

UNIVERSITY OF KANSAS

Jobina Khoo, M.S.

UNIVERSITY OF SOUTHERN MISSISSIPPI

By the time many of our students reached the advanced courses in our University's programs, they had a strong understanding of what methods of instruction fit best with their need to comprehend material. For students in our face-to-face courses, it was often easier to read facial expressions and body language and we could perceive whether they were grasping the information. However, for students in our distance education courses, it was much more important to present content in multiple ways. Creating variations in how content is presented would allow students in our distance education classrooms to interact with material in a way that made sense to meet their learning needs. Ultimately, this would create a level learning environment when comparing our face-to-face and distance education learners.

Multiple Means of Representation in Distance Education

The representation of content, particularly at a distance, is critical in order to provide clarity and to avoid miscommunication or misunderstanding; especially, when the goals, expectations, and purpose of the learning experience are represented to the learner. Simply put, we must purposefully design how we represent digital content in order to address the variability of the adult learner enrolled in the distance education learning experience. *Multiple Means of Representation* is the second of the three principles of Universal Design for Learning (UDL) framework, focusing on the manner in which we represent knowledge and information to the learner. **Figure 1** provides the specific breakdown of the *Multiple Means of Representation* principle using its three accompanying guidelines and twelve checkpoints.

UDL principle of representation is centered on the "what" of learning (Hall, Meyer, and Rose, 2012). The "what" is simply how students perceive and comprehend information which is foundational to the UDL principle of representation. As educators design instructional materials, our focus when planning should be the idea that students are highly variable in how they comprehend information (e.g., Guideline 1: Provide Options for Perception), how they understand the language being presented (e.g., Guideline 2: Provide Options for Language, Mathematical Expressions, and Symbols), and how they develop a deeper understanding of the information being presented (e.g., Guideline 3: Provide Options for Comprehension). These guidelines and the accompanying checkpoints are applicable to any educational environment including distance education content and instruction. UDL guidelines and checkpoints are intended to offer flexibility to designers in the planning and development of curricular materials and the subsequent use of these materials for instruction and assessment (Hall, Meyer, and Rose, 2012). Representation is one area in which attempts to address all guidelines and checkpoints in the development stage leads to richer digital materials that will better address the needs of diverse learners (e.g., non-traditional students, students from diverse backgrounds, international students). As you develop coursework for the distance education environment, it is important to focus on these guidelines and checkpoints individually and collectively to ensure adequate preparation for representation of material. In regard to the principle of representation, we suggest each guideline or checkpoint is mandatory to consider as you prepare your online learning environment.

Before we go further, let's clarify the type of distance education environment we will discuss. Distance education has evolved through the years to include everything from a postal-based education course to those utilizing semantic web technologies (Anderson and Dron, 2010). Although there are many terms used to discuss this type of distance learning (online learning, web-based learning, etc.), we will focus on e-learning. E-learning refers to "electronically mediated asynchronous and synchronous communication for the purpose of constructing and confirming knowledge," (Garrison, 2011, p.2). Thus, as we go forward and discuss distance education, the focus is on e-learning in today's online educational efforts.

In the following chapter we will examine each of the UDL second principle, *Multiple Means of Representation* guidelines and checkpoints, as well as discuss applications and demonstrate how to apply these guidelines and checkpoints in a distance learning environment. We will examine the pedagogy of representation, best practices in distance education application, and challenges that may occur with application, as we will look at instructor behaviors that support Multiple Means of Representation, student and faculty interactions, tools, resources, and strategies. Finally, we will close with examples of Multiple Means of Representation in online coursework. While we will focus primarily on postsecondary environments, information and exemplars for K–12 environments may be used as well. Certainly, the principles of UDL apply to any level of distance education.

Representation through Required Accessibility

Representation of content and digital materials in a distance learning course often overlaps with accessibility considerations. This means distance education coursework is required to meet federal accessibility standards that seek to ensure all digital material is represented in a manner that allows for accessibility as defined in federal guidelines and related organizational policies. The rights of all users to access digital content within the distance learning experience precedes current e-learning delivery dating back to the Rehabilitation Act of 1973. For example, the amended Section 508 of the Workforce Rehabilitation Act of 1973 enhances access to broadband (e.g., distance learning) technology and services for individuals with disabilities (Hashey and Stahl, 2014). Additional standards have followed including the World Wide Web Consortium (W3C) accessibility guidelines for the W3C's Web Accessibility Initiative (WAI) and the International Digital Publishing Forum's (IDPF) EPUB content publication standards. Outside the United States the European Unified Approach for Accessible Lifelong Learning (EU4ALL) initiated the concept of accessible lifelong learning and the elimination of barriers to the interlinked worlds of education and work through the use of appropriate digital technologies (Greer and Deshler, 2013).

Representation of digital materials from an accessibility perspective means that users will be able to perceive, understand, navigate and interact with digital content, and they can contribute to the digital materials (Yesilada, Brajnik, Vigo, and Harper, 2012). Required federal guidelines promote various forms of representation of digital materials through design tips which include providing the text equivalent or closed captioning for animation and video content, color contrast as well as appropriate font size, transcripts of all audio and accompanying descriptions for any video, and frequent accessibility testing during and after the digital content development and overall course design. These features target alternate means in accessing the digital materials. The standards require an alternate format, for instance, supporting an audio file with a complete transcript or close captioning the audio portion of a video.

Varying the representation through accessibility concentrates on multiple formats but does not alter the learning demands of the digital material. For example, providing an accessible digital text (e.g., online textbook, digital text-based lesson) often requires formatting to allow for a text-to-speech application that automatically reads the text to individuals with print impairments (e.g., someone who is blind and cannot see the text). Accessibility, in this instance, does not require reducing the complexity of the text, identifying the critical elements such as main idea of the text, reducing the demands of content-specific vocabulary, enhancing fluency, or changing other supports that would address the learning and cognitive demands of the text. Thus, accessible digital materials for distance education are the first step in *Multiple Means of Representation*. The second principle of UDL extends simple accessible representation from what is available to the learner to what is appropriate to their specific learning needs, further supporting the learning process through the use of digital materials to varied learners.

Pedagogy, Representation, and Distance Education

Identifying how UDL's Multiple Means of Representation and distance education fit together can seem overly simple. Teaching through an online or virtual format requires planning and posting of materials. You might be thinking "Of course an instructor will use multiple forms when representing the material." However, such logic only addresses Guideline 2 Checkpoint 2.5, "illustrate through multiple media." For this reason, it is important to consider the pedagogical intersection of distance education and universal design for learning.

According to Anderson and Dron (2012) three major theories are utilized in distance education approaches: Cognitive Behavior Theory,

Social-Constructivist Theory, and Connectivism. These three approaches are summarized in **Table 4.1**. These three pedagogical approaches all intersect with UDL, as instruction can be teacher-directed, socially constructed, or self-directed. UDL provides a scientifically based framework, which guides the design and development of a flexible curriculum, inclusive and effective for all learners (Rose and Gravel, 2010). Pedagogy includes the methods by which teachers guide learners through the learning process. Rather than accepting only one pedagogical approach to learning, UDL is based on neuroscience suggesting that learners are highly variable and require multiple approaches to learning. UDL accepts that there is variability among classrooms of learners and within the individual themselves. Therefore, all three pedagogical approaches to distance education presented above have a place in the framework of UDL. Creating options for learners that are teacher-directed (structured learning delivered by the teacher for the acquisition of knowledge), socially-constructed (teacher and/or peer support to construct new learning), and self-directed learning (directing one's own journey through the materials and creating one's own outcome), are all part of this flexible framework of UDL. When designing materials to represent course content, all of these pedagogical approaches should be considered.

Understanding the three pedagogical approaches to distance education helps us see that we are not simply addressing the use of multiple media under the principle of *Multiple Means of Representation;* display, type, language, and format of media are important to ensure learners can actually access or use the content you have designed. However, the ultimate purpose of any curriculum is for students to learn. Options for comprehension become critical when you, as the instructor, must also plan for material that represents content from the acquisition stage through generalization to other areas. Ultimately, the role of UDL's principle of Multiple Means of Representation in distance education is to represent content in such a way that learners can effectively achieve and go beyond the outcomes identified by the instructor through the original goals of the course.

Best Practices in Multiple Means of Representation in Distance Education

As we covered earlier, distance education has been used since the late 1800s in the form of correspondence education and has blossomed into (predominately) online or web-based education (Meyer, 2014). This digital explosion continues to expand from desktops to laptops to tablet and mobile phone technology. The Campus Computing Project (2014) reported that in addition to utilizing web-based formats for computer access (desktop or laptop) more than 99 percent of public universities had invested in mobile apps as well. Distance education is a fast-paced field with improvements and changes happening every day (Green, 2014). The best practice today may be somewhat different in six months and will definitely be different in one year. However, some practices seem to keep pace with the ever-changing field. We will discuss those here. Best practices have been developed in the area of offering courses online, synchronously and asynchronously.

As most educators know, distance education programs have accreditation bodies that release standards used to inform and evaluate programs on recommended practices. The primary accreditation body for distance education in the United States is the Distance Education Accrediting Commission (DEAC), recognized by the Council for Higher Education Accreditation (CHEA) and/or the U.S. Department of Education (USDE) (http://www.chea.org/pdf/CHEA_USDE_AllAccred.pdf). Additional professional organizations research, recommend, and evaluate best practices including the Western Cooperative for Educational Telecommunications (WCET), Instructional Technology Council and the Society for Information Technology and Teacher Education (SITE). All have developed recommendations and guidelines for best practice in distance education.

In 2013, Hew and Cheung synthesized the recommended guidelines from nine organizations monitoring distance education. One theme identified across all nine organizations directly related to UDL Multiple Means of Representation is instructional design. We recommended the following practices for distance learning courses using both UDL Multiple Means of Representation checkpoints and guidelines as well as the synthesis of distance learning guidelines presented by Hew and Cheung (see **Table 4.2**).

Let's take a closer look at each of these through the lens of UDL Multiple Means of Representation.

Represent Basic Course Expectations through Multiple Means

Distance education courses are typically built in Learning Management Systems (LMS) for distribution to students in either a synchronous, asynchronous, or hybrid method. Course content is loaded into a platform for learners to access; similar to traditional courses, a course syllabus, objectives, assignments, resources, calendar, and other tools may be provided. Before an instructor thinks about how he or she is representing the actual content of the course, the instructor should invest time thinking about the representation of the course overall. Identifying barriers in how course expectations are represented is critical to ensuring all learners can access and use the course as represented. A syllabus, for example, is traditionally a static Word or pdf document. While an instructor may post a document for students to use, this would not be the best practice under UDL Representation. Basic principles of Universal Design (UD) should guide the development and representation of a course syllabus to include pictures and/or videos of the instructor; a course tour; links for objectives, resources for using the LMS, resources for the course, and accommodations if needed; and a variety of contact information for the instructor (Thomson, Fichten, Havel, Budd, and Asuncion, 2015). UDL Universe through the Enact Project at Sonoma State provides a detailed rubric to evaluate your course syllabus under a UDL framework (http://lgdata.s3-website-us-east-1.amazonaws.com/docs/2205/451064/UDL_Syllabus_Rubric_UPDATED_2-9-2012.pdf). Ensuring your course expectations are represented through multiple means, in accessible formats, following the UDL guidelines of perception, options for language, and options for comprehension is a critical first step in designing a quality distance learning course.

Beyond the initial syllabus, instructors and the developers of distance learning need to appreciate the confines of most distance education learning experiences. For example, fully online asynchronous distance learning courses have a number of essential elements that structure the learning experience. First, the course is developed to be available or accessible twenty-four hours a day, seven days a week. The availability of the course is meant to be flexible for the varying needs of the learner. Constant access often leads to components that are not aligned with the idea of Multiple Means of Representation. That is, the LMS requires a structure or an approach that is controlled requiring a sequence of learning experiences to ensure independence on the part of the learner, allowing them to work at his or her own level and pace without an instructor's immediate response and direction. As such, the standard class is a set of readings or presentations in which the students read and watch digital material. While these readings and presentations might be designed to be accessible (e.g., text-to-speech, closed captioning for the video) the representation of the content has a standard for each learning module of experience. Likewise, instruction is often followed by a traditional assessment that uses multiple choice questions or similar response items that are scored automatically, allowing the student an immediate understanding of his or her progress and an ability to move forward with the remaining content without instructor review and scoring. Again, accessibility options such as having the test items read out loud and various manners in which the item could be displayed should be provided (e.g., images to further represent an idea). The reality is that the assessment remains in a primary mode of representation. This limits how information can be displayed, formatted, and/or scaffold for the student. It also limits the options that could be offered to the learner allowing him or her variability in illustrating competence in a content area.

The packaging of distance education through a prescribed LMS fosters limited options for representation. For example, the well-meaning instructor seeks to offer a variety of assessment options but is often limited by his or her LMS. In using the LMS, the assessments conform to a certain structure (e.g., multiple choice, essay question) limiting the variability in how the question and/or information is represented to the learner. Therefore, the representation of the initial instructional content can often be controlled by the functionality of the LMS. While the LMS offers the option to upload digital materials, the systems reinforce digital materials that are formatted in particular ways (e.g., pdfs, Word docs) fostering limited options for the instructor to provide and for the student to use.

Finally, the common approach of how we offer distance education fosters a learning experience that is often limiting based on the representation of the ideas and content. Limits are set because many distance education courses are taught by multiple instructors. One semester it may be instructor X, followed by instructor Y, with instructor Z assisting every summer. The variety of instructors often facilitates a distance education experience that is structured into a box, creating a learning experience that is packaged into instructional units tied to particular learning or professional standards. Each learning module presents the information and then assesses student understanding, measures the learning outcomes, and then offers the next sequence in the learning experience. The course instructor, who facilitates or manages the distance education experience, is restricted as to information or content he or she can modify or alter due to the consistency of material provided from multiple instructors. The packaging then limits the learning options and curtails the Multiple Means of Representation one might seek to further include with the digital materials.

Media Should Allow Options for Navigation, Use, and Application by Learners

To make sure content is represented under a UDL framework and following best practices for distance learning, an instructor's first consideration should be to determine if those materials meet basic accessibility guidelines for digital materials. UDL Guideline I.1 Options for Perception, including auditory, visual, and customized displays of information are critical to ensuring best practice here. Additionally, checkpoints under UDL Guideline I.2 Options for Language, Mathematical Expressions and Symbols are also critically important to consider when designing materials. Principles of Accessible Design are provided by WebAIM (n.d.) http://webaim.org/intro/#principles.

Determining accessibility of the digital materials is the initial step. As mentioned, accessibility offers physical and sensory representation options but often does not provide variability for the cognitive demands of the material. Thus, identifying an accessible textbook should be followed by determining the manner in which the text is supported for learner variability. For example, when selecting digital reading materials (e.g., course textbook) Multiple Means of Representation would take into consideration a number of factors. First, can the digital text be accessible through a text-to-speech tool allowing the learner to read the text, listen to the text being read to them, highlight the word or sentence being read, control for the volume rate, and digital voice of the reading. While textbook publishers are increasingly offering accessibility options, distance education instructors are responsible for reviewing the digital reading material they assign. If options are limited, the instructor should work to identify (with the assistance of LMS facilitators or other course design personnel) tools that could be used by the learners (e.g., Chrome text-to-speech Apps, Adobe Reader tools).

Next, instructors need to identify the learning supports embedded within the digital readings to support meaning, represent the main idea, and allow the learner to further engage in the digital material. These supports could be a variety of features such as embedded scaffolds, graphic organizers that visually map out the content, and similar features. Finally, Multiple Means of Representation requires content represented through text be further represented through images, graphics, figures, audio, and potentially video that allows for the learner struggling with the demands of text-based content the ability to gain an understanding of the material through multiple means. These provisions extend the learning experience by allowing the student a foundation from which to build. In a distance learning educational experience, the text provided in Multiple Means of Representation should be one of several options learners can aquire knowledge on a particular idea or concept. Content and structure of class should be scaffolded to supply learner supports towards comprehension, allowing access at their entry level and promotion to higher order thinking skills.

The representation of instructional content and materials utilizing learning strategies that support growth in comprehension at different levels is critically important when designing distance learning. While accessibly designed content is fundamentally important, it is equally important to ensure that once students have gained access to course content, instructional strategies support the representation of those materials in ways promote comprehension. In their synthesis of guidelines for distance learning, Hew and Cheung (2013) discuss the need for the utilization of instructional strategies that demonstrate the application of content (e.g., models procedures applied in context), the analysis of content (breaking content down into parts and demonstrating the relationship of those parts to each other and the whole), the synthesis of content (pulling the pieces together to create a whole), and evaluation of content (making judgements of quality). UDL Guideline I.3 is most helpful for consideration here. Checkpoints under UDL Guideline I.3 Providing Options for Comprehension include the following:

3.1 Activate or supply background knowledge
3.2 Highlight patterns, critical features, big ideas, and relationships
3.3 Guide information processing, visualization, and manipulation
3.4 Maximize transfer and generalization

For example, the face-to-face lecture in the distance education experience is often represented in several mediums. The traditional format is to simply transfer the face-to-face presentation (e.g., PowerPoint) to the online class, allowing students to download the slides and related notes. Yes, students have access to the material; however, from an instructional perspective, limited options are presented for representation. One should ask how is this different from any assigned reading in respect to the material the student is accessing. Instead, to maximize comprehension and build upon the learning experience for subsequent generalization, instructors in the distance education environment could utilize a number of technology tools and instructional practices. These could include:

- An interactive presentation that mixes visual slides with interactive graphics, embedded audio, a visual map of the learning

experience, and embedded video or interactive graphics to illustrate a concept (e.g., Prezi).
- An interactive timeline that embeds information on the concept, contextual reference to when it occurred and within what setting, embedded media to further illustrate the happening, and a visual sequence to offer order of the events.
- A series of interactive presentations that chunk ideas through audio, visual, text, and graphic representation (e.g., audio or video podcasts).
- Case-based or problem-based learning scenarios that offer students an opportunity to explore the material and learning concepts. Applying simulations and augmenting the experience through virtual-reality apps and web-based tools could further foster understanding and subsequent application.

Although not mentioned directly, it is also critically important to think about representation in your evaluation and assessment materials. Assessment should be an accurate evaluation of what was taught (Salvia, Ysseldyke, and Whitmer, 2012). The purpose of assessment is to find out if the learner did or did not achieve the learning target. Your assessments should be represented in ways that directly reflect the learning target and the materials or content used with learners. All three representation guidelines apply to the development of assessments. It is important that assessments be adaptable to learner's audio, visual, and display needs; provide options for language, symbols, vocabulary, mathematical expressions; and provide options for measuring comprehension that evaluates main ideas, relationships, transfer, and generalization.

Each of the UDL representation checkpoints align with best practices in distance instruction focused on application, analysis, synthesis and evaluation. By following these practices when designing your course layout and curriculum, you can design a course that "gives all individuals equal opportunity to learn" (National Center on Universal Design for Learning, http://www.udlcenter.org/aboutudl).

Challenges to Multiple Means of Representation in Distance Education

Using the UDL framework to guide the representation of content and materials in the development of an online course does not come without challenges. Distance education provides its own challenges. The most significant challenge of distance education is the very nature of the changing technology. Since the emergence of technology as a classroom application in 1970, the fast-paced technological advancements have been increasingly challenging for educators who are not technological experts to keep pace (Cox, 2013). Knowing how to effectively identify, use, and maintain programs, software, applications, communication tools, etc. requires constant effort for anyone implementing technology in his/her classroom (online or otherwise). Staying abreast of the latest technology is one of the most significant challenges to distance education. Meyer (2014) suggests age, ability to collaborate, preparedness, and consideration of content as well as delivery systems are all critical factors in delivering online coursework successfully. Designing your course and curriculum using the latest technology to display, engage, or communicate with learners is challenging, however, not impossible.

For the instructor, an essential practice is to consider the instructional goal and effective strategies and to inquire on the innovations that allow one to extend that practice in the distance education environment. For example, if peer-to-peer interaction is critical to foster a collaborative learning experience, distance education instructors can often look to the course LMS for solutions. LMS will generally offer tools for virtual student interaction. These could be blogs, discussion forums, group chats, virtual rooms where students can post, upload, or download relevant materials, as well as a host of other digital tools that foster peer interaction. Of course, examining these tools through the Multiple Means of Representation lens will extend the learning options for all learners and potentially assist the distance instructor's decision making process as they seek to identify the appropriate tools. By combining the distance learning tools with principle two, learners can use the blog, for instance, to share ideas, post videos, include audio files, share a link that illustrates an instructional process, and the list continues. For the instructor, selecting the right tools and facilitating the peer-to-peer interaction with the varied means of representation fosters effective interactions and furthers an inclusive learning experience for the entire class.

A second and equally significant challenge surrounds pedagogy in distance educational environments. Distance education instructors often believe they address many basic issues of access through default, meaning they assume digital materials allow for changes in display, auditory or visual options as required by Guideline 1.1: Options for Perception. It is important to evaluate each representation of content to ensure there are no barriers presented in the perception or display of these materials. Some digital materials allow options for language, mathematical expressions, and symbols as required by Guideline 1.2. Fewer digital materials provide options for comprehension as required by Guideline 1.3. Pedagogy, content knowledge, and comprehension are all interrelated (Loughran, 2013). The application of the UDL framework in a distance educational environment requires faculty to be instructional designers, content experts, and technology specialists. Representation of content that leads to a more learner-centric model is necessary to extend the use of technology from information delivery to critical comprehension of material (Meyer, 2014).

This is especially true with the increased use of video that introduces concepts, reinforces an idea, and/or simply illustrates an element of instruction. The caution with video is to understand that all videos are not created equal. Like any digital material, video-based resources need to be comprehended by the learner. There is a level of cognitive load whereby the student will need to identify the purpose of the video, the main ideas, the structure of what is being shared, and how to take note of this information, structure for future reference, and apply to the instructional event at hand. With this in mind, identifying a YouTube resource might extend beyond simply searching for a video, finding it, and linking it to the instructional experience for the distance education experience. Instead, there is a significant review process needed when one considers the resource and what it seeks to represent, what the visual illustration demands of the learner (e.g., background knowledge), what additional supports are needed for the learner to benefit from the video, and similar questions. For the K–12 learning experience, BrainPop (see brainpop.com), a web-based and app-based tool, is a good example of a resource that represents ideas and information by setting the stage for the learner and representing concepts through print, explanation, audio, and visuals all wrapped into a video-based experience.

There are challenges to teaching online using the UDL framework. However, these challenges are not impossible to navigate. Advanced planning of content and instructional goals, up-to-date professional development in technological tools and advancements, and constant evaluation of effectiveness can lead to less difficulty in the application of distance education.

Resources

Many resources are available to support the application of the UDL Framework including Multiple Means of Representation. Additionally, many tools are available to support representation of content in many formats. **Table 4.3** provides a list of those resources.

Conclusion

The purpose of this chapter was to discuss the application of the UDL principle Multiple Means of Representation to distance education. We have presented pedagogy, best practices, challenges, and resources supporting the application of UDL Multiple Means of Representation in distance education environments.

References

Anderson, T., and Dron, J. (2010). "Three generations of distance education pedagogy." *The International Review of Research in Open and Distributed Learning*, 12(3), 80–97.

Anderson, T., and Dron, J. (2012). "Learning technology through three generations of technology enhanced distance education pedagogy." *European Journal of Open, Distance and E-learning*, 15(2).

CAST (2011). *Universal Design for Learning Guidelines*, version 2.0. Wakefield, MA: Author.

Chan, S. (2010). "Designing an online class using a constructivist approach." *Journal of Adult Education*, 39(1), 26–39.

Cox, M. J. (2013). "Formal to informal learning with IT: Research challenges and issues for e-learning." *Journal of Computer Assisted Learning*, 29(1), 85–105.

Garrison, D. R. (2011). *E-learning in the 21st Century: A Framework for Research and Practice.* Taylor and Francis.

Green, K. C. (2014). "The 2014 national survey of computer and information technology in U.S. higher education." *The Campus Computing Project.* Retrieved from http://www.campuscomputing.net/item/campus-computing-2014.

Greer, D., and Deshler, D. (2013). "Looking at online learning through the accessibility lens." *Better: Evidence-based Education*, 5(3), 16–17. Retrieved from http://www.betterevidence.org/issue-13/looking-at-online-learning-through-the-accessibility-lens/.

Hall, T. E., Meyer, A., and Rose, D. H. (2012). "Universal design for learning in the classroom." In K. R. Harris and S. Graham (Eds.), *Practical Applications*, 156.

Hashey, A., and Stahl, S. (2014). "Making online learning accessible for students with disabilities." *Teaching Exceptional Children*, 46(5), 70–78.

Hew, K. F., and Cheung, W. S. (2013). "Designing and implementing e-learning courses: A comparative analysis of policy guidelines from nine professional organizations." *International Journal of e-Education, e-Business, e-Management and e-Learning*, 3(3), 178.

Kop, R. (2011). "The challenges to connectivist learning on open online networks: Learning experiences during a massive open online course." *The International Review of Research in Open and Distributed Learning*, 12(3), 19–38.

Loughran, J. (2013). "Pedagogy: Making sense of the complex relationship between teaching and learning." *Curriculum Inquiry*, 43(1), 118–141.

Meyer, K. A. (2014). "Quality in distance education: focus on on-line learning." *ASHE-ERIC Higher Education Report*. Jossey-Bass Higher and Adult Education Series.

Rose, D. H., and Gravel, J. W. (2010). "Universal design for learning." In P. Peterson, E. Baker, and B. McGraw (Eds). *International Encyclopedia of Education* (pp.119–124). Oxford, UK: Elsevier.

Salvia, J., Ysseldyke, J., and Witmer, S. (2012). *Assessment: In Special and Inclusive Education*. Cengage Learning.

Siemens, G. (2007). "Connectivism: Creating a learning ecology in distributed environments." In T. Hug (Ed.), *Didactics of Microlearning: Concepts, Discourses and Examples*. Munster, Germany: Waxmann Verlag.

Thomson, R., Fichten, C. S., Havel, A., Budd, J., and Asuncion, J. (2015). "Blending universal design, e-learning, and information and communication technologies." *Universal Design in Higher Education: From Principles to Practice*, 275–284.

Appendices

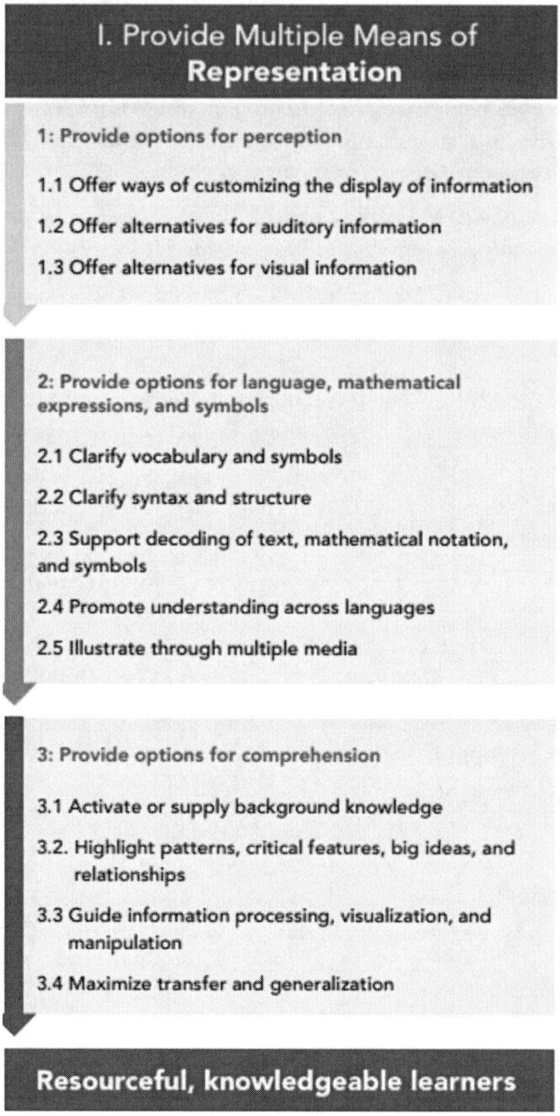

Figure 4.1: Multiple Means of Representation

Adapted from "Universal Design for Learning Guidelines," by CAST (2011). Universal Design for Learning Guidelines, *version 2.0. Wakefield, MA: Author. Copyright 2011 by CAST.*

Table 4.1: Three Major Approaches to Distance Education

	Three Theoretical Approaches to Distance Education		
	Cognitive Behavior	Social-Constructivist	Connectivism
Main Theorists	• Dick • Carey	• Vgotsky • Dewey	• Siemens
Best Use	• Teacher-guided individual instruction of new material.	• Teacher-guided discussion with student integration.	• Learner-guided exploration, creation, and dissemination of new work.
Key Points	• Teacher-directed learning • Delivery of knowledge through represented content • Learner required to access and respond individually • Evaluation through recall-type assessment • Instructor designed course content • Organization begins with the identification of instructional goals and ends with summative evaluation of learner • Learning activities: ◦ Text ◦ Video ◦ Multi-media materials • Dick and Carey model of instructional design: ◦ http://www.instructionaldesign.org/models/dick_carey_model.html.	• Integrated teacher-student learning • Integration of new knowledge with previous experiences with support from instructor • Human-communication based model for interactive environments • Five design principles: ◦ Pose problems of emerging relevance to students ◦ Structure learning around primary concepts ◦ Seek and validate students' point of view ◦ Adapt curriculum to address students' suppositions ◦ Assess student learning in the context of teaching ◦ Challenging in distance education	• Self-directed learning • Learner being connected to a series of networks • Learner can add to and take away from networks as he or she learns • Four activities: ◦ Aggregation ◦ Relation ◦ Creation ◦ Sharing • Bottom-up design • Does not work well when the goal of the course is to teach a specific skill or knowledge content

Table 4.2: UDL Multiple Means of Presentation with Hew and Cheung's Synthesis of Distance Learning Guidelines

UDL	Hew and Cheung
Multiple Means of Representation	Synthesis of Distance Learning
1. Provide options for perception 1.1 Offer ways of customizing the display of information 1.2 Offer alternatives for auditory information 1.3 Offer alternatives for visual information	• Course expectations/information • Learning objectives • Instructional strategy
2. Provide options for language, mathematical expressions, and symbols 2.1 Clarify vocabulary and symbols 2.2 Clarify syntax and structure 2.3 Support decoding of text, mathematical notation 2.4 Promote understand across languages 2.5 Illustrate through multiple media	• Use of media and learning styles • Student–instructor interaction • Instructional strategy
3. Provide options for comprehension 3.1 Activate or supply background knowledge 3.2 Highlight patterns, critical features, big ideas, and relationships 3.3 Guide information processing visualization, and manipulation 3.4 Maximize transfer and generalization	• Student–student interaction • Student collaboration • Use of media and learning styles • Instructional strategy

Table 4.3: Online UDL Resources

Resource	Resource Information	Resource Website
Animoto	• Web-based and app tool • Video design through the use of slides, photos, graphics, and images • Creates a video	https://animoto.com
Authorstream	• Interactive presentation experience • Offers the essential slide and features tools • Embed the slides into a live broadcast, multiple video formats, or uploads to video channels like YouTube	http://www.authorstream.com
Cast	• UDL website • Provides free, robust learning tools • Offers accessible educational materials	www.cast.org
Enact Project UDL Universe	• Support for postsecondary • Provides resources and examples for UDL implementation	http://enact.sonoma.edu/udl
Google Drive	• Storage resource for distance education • Creates a place to structure presentation (e.g., Google Presentation), resources (e.g., Google docs), and any additional digital resources • Allows file sharing • Create a repository of materials for review and use	https://drive.google.com
National Center on UDL	• UDL website • Provides UDL resources • Provides media presentation to help educators understand and implement UDL skills	http://www.udlcenter.org

Table 4.3: continued

Resource	Resource Information	Resource Website
Prezi	• Interactive presentation system • Presents ideas and links critical concepts that are further defended through the individual slides	https://prezi.com
Projeqt	• Presentation platform combined with a story-telling experience • Allows an instructor to share information in a story structure	http://www.projeqt.com
Slidebean	• Presentation systems • Allows material to be presented in a singular format and embedded into their system for an interactively designed slide • Expands how the material is represented	http://slidebean.com
Slideshare	• Presentation experience online • Takes traditional files (e.g., PDF, Word doc) and uploads them into an interactive platform • Creates a slideshow experience allowing another option for the representation of the material	http://www.slideshare.net
UDL IRN	• UDL Implementation and Research Network • Provides UDL resources for teachers	http://udl-irn.org
UDL on Campus	• Focuses on higher education • Specific element of CAST • Provides course design • Materials and media for learning environments	http://udloncampus.cast.org/home#.VwwAYZwrKUk
Wideo	• Online video development • Takes the basics of PPT and expands what can be developed with animated videos	http://wideo.co/en/

5

Multiple Means of Expression

Kimberly Coy

CALIFORNIA STATE UNIVERSITY, FRESNO

I was once a kindergarten teacher, and I was terrified. During my pre-service teaching experiences I always felt the kindergarten rooms were to be avoided at all cost. They were the rooms that made you sticky! They were the rooms where parents were "involved." The kindergarten rooms required lots of happy smiles, an ability to draw animals, and a love of crafts. None of those skills came naturally to me. Imagine my terror at being assigned a full day kindergarten classroom at the beginning of my teaching career. The good news is we all survived and thrived. The students learned how to use the big kid bathrooms, the parents learned their children were gifted with clay, and I learned to sing out loud. I also discovered that the ability to express learning came in many forms. For in kindergarten, students show what they know with their whole wiggly, sticky bodies! As I taught older grades, then post secondary students, and unexpectedly in digital environments, I have strived to bring the kindergarten love of expression with me. This is a commitment to offering multiple forms of expression so students can demonstrate what they know, and I can understand and reflect on my teaching practices toward improvement.

Expression in Distance Education

How do instructors know that the goals and objectives in a lesson, unit, or course have been met? They know because the student demonstrates knowledge of the goals and objectives to the instructors' satisfaction. By employing a Universal Design for Learning (UDL) lens students or learners in all educational environments have many options to demonstrate knowledge and understanding. However, in a distance learning environment providing high quality options for expression can seem difficult, and it is certainly different from a face-to-face classroom. (Rose, Harbour, Johnston, Daley, and Abarbanell, L. 2006). The purpose of this chapter is to tackle the challenge of expression in distance learning by exploring helpful tools, resources, and strategies that provide multiple ways action and expression can work in digital environments.

This chapter has been organized into three sections. The first is a brief literature review. It is essential to look at the work of other educators in the field of distance learning as it evolves so quickly. Second, the chapter will look at action and expression in digital course design with the lens of Universal Design for Learning (UDL) to spotlight specific strategies to provide multiple means of action and expression. The goal is to encourage strategic, goal-directed learners (Meyer and Rose, 2005). Finally, there are two tables providing specific resources and examples educators can use in digital environments to provide options for action and expression. These tables are organized around the UDL guidelines and checkpoints. Definition of terms used in this chapter:

- Learner—Also known and referred to as the student.
- Application—Can be a program or an "app" on a computer or smart device.
- Virtual—In reference to school. Also referred to as distance or online.

Literature Review

Teaching and learning in online environments differs from teaching and learning in traditional face-to-face settings. While classrooms in brick and mortar schools may look different physically, in the virtual world physical differences in the classroom are mitigated. At first glance the virtual classroom may seem two-dimensional. This perception can be a barrier. In addition, infrastructure limitations and hardware associated with virtual environments can act as learning barriers by negatively impacting the tone and volume quality of voices in the class, clarity of visual stimuli, and pace of the class. Pauses in communication or lapses between voice and visual displays can lead to frustration for both teachers and students, as can untimely instructor responses and ambiguous directions regarding teacher and student responsibilities during assignments (Capdeferro and Romero, 2012; Hodges and Cowan, 2012; Tempelaar et al., 2011). In addition, Vasquez et al., (2011), in case studies of virtual classroom settings, pointed out that numerous challenges exist when teachers attempt to manage student behavior at a distance. Hawkins, Graham, and Barbour (2012) pointed out that some teachers experience a sense of disconnection from students, fellow virtual teachers, and traditional notions of teaching.

Despite these challenges, online teachers must facilitate meaningful student communication and interactions. Im and Lee (2003–2004) and Borup, West, and Graham (2011) demonstrated that synchronous discussions could promote social interactions among learners and have a substantial impact on establishing instructors' social presence. Hou and Wu (2011) and Cook, Annetta, Dickerson, and Minogue (2011) presented similar findings, noting that participants in synchronous discussions and text chats created social interactions that participants perceived as more reflective, interactive, and supportive than those in asynchronous environments.

Asynchronous discussion allowed for more task-oriented outcomes. This may be of particular relevance to students because it allows teachers to maximize students' strengths and engagement opportunities (i.e., social interaction) while providing remedial support as necessary during task completion. Hines and Pearl (2004) purported that a balance of synchronous and asynchronous experiences are necessary to support a variety of communication patterns among students. Several researchers (e.g., Bower and Hedberg, 2010; Marchand and Gutierrez, 2012; Hwang and Yang, 2008) noted that student interaction and collaboration could occur effectively online. In addition, Lowes (2007) noted that teachers must be able to use new technologies effectively, manage costs, and mentor newer teachers within communities of practice.

Students with a wide variety of cognitive, physical, social, and behavioral skills are increasingly participating in online learning. Unfortunately, there is limited research examining the types of instruction that are necessary to maximize student learning in online K–8 environments. It is important to highlight issues identified in the literature that impact today's classroom teachers, discuss the results from a recent study that examined Universal Design for Learning during online synchronous lessons, and propose instructional strategies that have the potential to enhance student outcomes during online instruction. Interviews with leaders in existing virtual schools highlight the challenges and concerns facing special education teachers and the industry. Implications for professional development activities also are discussed (Coy, Marino, and Serianni, 2014).

Distance educational environments attract a wide variety of students at the university level as well as high school and even elementary virtual school settings (Gemen, Pape, Vashaw, and Watson, 2015). Students who have learning differences who attend school in the virtual environment encounter different barriers and opportunities for academic growth. The role parents take in facilitating schooling activities can be dramatically increased. Therefore, professional development in a virtual school differs from brick and mortar schools in part because of parent roles. The skills of the parents as educational partners needs to be considered so the parental role can provide tools and strategies to support the students' education on a continual basis (Coy and Hirschmann, 2014).

Action and Expression in Distance Education Design

Planning for Universal Design in course development reduces but may not eliminate the need for accommodations for students with disabilities. Burgstahler (2013) uses the example of having a sign language interpreter at the ready only for classes where there is a student who needs one. Burgstahler also identifies a seven-step process to adapt universal design for instruction. The seven steps are: 1. Identify the course; 2. Define the universe; 3. Involve students; 4. Adopt instructional strategies; 5. Apply instructional strategies; 6. Plan for accommodations; and 7. Evaluate (Burgstahler, 2014). When focusing on student expression "involve students" can steer course designers in a positive direction. For example Burgstahler identifies this step in the following way: "Consider perspectives of students with diverse characteristics. . . ." (p. 24) Reaching out to students themselves as well as looking at the demographics of the learning population the course is serving can be a valuable way to plan for learner expression.

Within a recent research study looking for UDL in synchronous online lessons, (Coy, Marino, and Serianni, 2014) one finding points out that teachers, instructors, and educational designers need to invite a wide range of expressive behaviors from learners. When a range of action and expression options is provided, learners will engage and use these options within the design frame. First, identify Barriers to Action and Expression in the learning environment. Inherent in all learning environments are barriers. These barriers can be unique to individual settings, students, or a product of the technology. Instructors can begin by taking specific inventory of the physical environment and notice the all too often barriers provided in many classrooms. For example, in face-to-face classrooms barriers can range from the overhead lighting (that reduces most humans to one-dimensional versions of themselves), to the desks that were not built to accommodate laptops or power up any device. What can be done to overcome these barriers? Advocating for a change of classroom might work. Another option may include having students group desks together to form makeshift tables, letting students sit on the floor, bringing in alternative lighting, or turning off the overhead lights altogether.

Online courses come with barriers that instructors can inventory as well. One may be the online learning platform (OLS) the university provides. A particular OLS may be new to the institution or very complicated. A way to break down this barrier is to create or use an existing tutorial for the specific OLS. Allowing a tutorial to be the beginning part of the online course, with course credits or points, helps to mitigate this barrier for students. Important to remember with a barrier inventory is that learners should be expected to contribute to this process. What is a perceived barrier for one learner is not for another. A robust discussion of barriers and their eliminations are an important part of any course.

Begin with the end in mind. Goals and objectives are the constructs, knowledge, skills, or abilities that are measured by assessments. Instructors should continually evaluate the assessment required of students and consider that irrelevant factors may impede accurate assessment of individual student knowledge, skills, and abilities. For example, differences in organization and time management, or background skills and knowledge, could result in inaccurate measurement of student's abilities on course objectives.

Traditional discussions are an identifiable barrier for many students in online courses. Because peer-to-peer learning is so important (Vasquez and Serianni, 2012) it is necessary to reduce this barrier. Plan for a variety of ways for students to interact. Here are some specific ideas:

- Use Zoom (www.zoom.com) for planned synchronous instruction. This is a low-cost interactive tool that participants join through a website, and students can see each other's facial expressions.
- Create a Facebook page that is open only to the students in the course. Have students react to course content by assigning postings, (written, images, videos, graphic organizers) and then assign students to comment on each others posts.
- GIFs are all about expression. To learn about GIFs go to Facebook, message a friend, click on GIF button, type in the idea "have a good day" and you can send an expression immediately. Better yet, have students create their own GIF's to send to each other or the instructor to express ideas and reactions to content.

Provide Options for Physical Action

Even in the digital world there is physical action. For example, learners need to be able to physically navigate a laptop, tablet, or smart phone in order to be able to express their ideas and thoughts through these devices. Instructors need to make sure learners are able to use these devices without physical barriers and without information barriers. For example, if assignments are in one form only, like a traditional paper, this may provide students a narrow way to express if they have reached understanding of the goal. By providing alternatives for participation during class time and study time instructors are more likely to get a better response toward the educational goal. In face-to-face classrooms during lectures, presentations, or class discussions teachers might encourage students to join in whole group discussions, chat in small groups or with one other student, or even to journal privately. In digital classrooms to access technology provides options for student expression. This can be accomplished by using texting, voice, video, e-mail, Facebook message, Skype, etc. Additional specific examples for student options include:

- Encouraging students to make a short video for an assignment using iMovie.
- Teaching students how to create a Voki.
- Asking students to give a tour of their study area during a synchronous lesson or meeting using the video option.

Provide Options for Expression and Communication

Strive for effective alternative assessments based on goals and objectives. One type of expression is not equally suited to every student, or every goal. The current free or low cost opportunities for learners to express themselves are practically unlimited. As an instructor or educational designer do not assume students know how to use enough of these options to make deep choices. Provide new resources for expression and teach learners how to use the specific resources, and ask students to generate resources to share with the class. Here are some great examples:

- Vimeo—an easy way to make online videos.
  Free for basic. www.vimeo.com.
- Prezi—presentation software.
  Free for basic. www.prezi.com.
- Glogster—creates multi-media posters.
  Small fee. www.glogster.com.

Provide Options for Executive Functions

Instructors should use meta-cognitive goals transparently by explaining instructor thinking around the choices of both content and assessment. For example, when telling a story to illustrate a concept, make a point of telling the students that storytelling is an option for multiple means of representation or expression. The digital world offers almost too many choices in new applications and programs. Students need a way to judge what options work for them, and a way to match the application with the assignment. Teachers need to provide instruction to support learner choices. This does not mean that the teacher needs to have mastery of each option, but instead is willing to learn alongside students in making judgments. Specific examples include:

- Give the class choices for an assignment that reflects on interacting with new content, i.e., a book chapter, journal article, or lecture; iMovie, PowerPoint with voiceover, or Voki. Included in the assignment is a reflection piece on the effectiveness of their choice of expression. Share the reflections with the whole class.
- Create a rubric for students to use when choosing applications for expression.
- Assign small groups of students to create a rubric to use when choosing applications for expression.

Specific resources tied to UDL checkpoints are provided in **Table 5.1.**

Table 5.1: Actionable UDL

Actionable UDL	Specific Tools and Resources
Providing options for physical action by: • Varying the method for response and navigation. • Optimizing access to tools and assistive technologies.	Facebook, www.facebook.com Skype, www.skype.com Voki, www.voki.com Zoom, https://zoom.us GIFs, http://makeagif.com Graphic Organizers, https://www.teachervision.com/graphic-organizers/printable/6293.html ShowMe, http://www.showme.com

Table 5.1: continued

Actionable UDL	Specific Tools and Resources
Provide options for expression and communication by: • Using multiple media for communication. • Using multiple tools for construction and composition. • Building fluencies with graduated levels of support for practice and performance.	Vimeo, https://vimeo.com YouTube, https://www.youtube.com Prezi, https://prezi.com PowerPoint with voiceover, http://www.emergingedtech.com/2012/12/add-voice-over-to-powerpoint-presentations-in-5-easy-steps/ Glogster, http://www.glogster.com/#love Nearpod, http://www.nearpod.com/index.php Explain Everything, http://explaineverything.com
Provide options for executive functions by: • Guiding appropriate goal-setting. • Supporting planning and strategy development. • Facilitating managing information and resources. • Enhancing capacity for monitoring progress.	Power Point, http://presentationsoft.about.com/od/powerpoint101/a/begin_guide.htm Voki, www.voki.com Smore, https://www.smore.com Canva, https://www.canva.com Socrative, http://www.socrative.com Edmodo, https://www.edmodo.com UDL On Campus: Universal Design for Learning in Higher Education—a guide CAST, http://udloncampus.cast.org/home#.VE6ccRCF9vk

Back to kindergarten, this time in the digital world. A colleague of mine reported this story to the staff while we were both working for a fully online K–12 public school. She was engaging with a small group of four or five kindergarten students on a math lesson. Each student was in their own home, in front of their computers with the camera on. The teacher could see each of them, and they could all see each other. Everyone had some manipulative (blocks, etc.) with them, and the students were using these to solve a mathematical problem. Suddenly, a door opened behind one of the students and a man walks out of what was clearly the bathroom and all he was wearing was a towel. Most of his birthday suit was exposed. My friend started to freak out. She was so shocked that by the time she realized she should turn off that student's camera the whole event was over. This is the type of story that can only happen online. What really surprised her was that not one student seemed to notice! Gotta love kindergarten!

References

Borup, J., West, R. E., and Graham, C. R. (2012). "Improving online social presence through asynchronous video." *Internet and Higher Education,* 15, 195–203.

Bower, M., and Hedberg, M. (2010). "A quantitative multimodal discourse analysis of teaching and learning in a Web-conferencing environment—the efficacy of student-centered learning designs." *Computers and Education,* 54, 462–478.

Burgstahler, S. E. and Cory, R. C. (Eds). (2013). *Universal Design in Higher Education.* Massachusetts: Harvard Education Press.

Capdeferro, N., and Romero, M. (2010). "Are online learners frustrated with collaborative learning experiences?" *The International Review of Research in Open and Distance Learning, 13(2),* 26–44. Retrieved from http://www.irrodl.org/index.php/irrodl/article/view/1127.

Cook, M., Annetta, L. A., Dickerson, D. L., and Minogue, J. (2011). "In-service teachers' perceptions on online learning environments." *The Quarterly Review of Distance Education,* 12(2), 73–79.

Coy, K., and Hirschmann, K. (2014). "Professional development for special education teachers in virtual schools." *International Journal of Dyslexia,* 40(1), 17–23.

Coy, K, Marino, M. T., and Serianni, B. (2014). "Using Universal Design for Learning in synchronous online instruction." *Journal of Special Education Technology,* 29(1), 63–74.

Gemen, B., Pape, L., Vashaw, L., and Watson, J. (2015). *Keeping Pace with K–12 Online Digital: An Annual Review of Policy and Practice.* Mountain View CA: The Evergreen Group.(4).

Hawkins, A., Graham, C. R., and Barbour, M. K. (2011). "'Everybody is their own island': Teacher disconnection in a virtual school." *The International Review of Research in Open and Distance Learning,* 13(2), 124–144. Retrieved from http://www.irrodl.org/index.php/irrodl/article/view/967.

Hines, R. A., and Pearl, C. E. (2004). "Increasing interaction in Web-based instruction: Using synchronous chats and asynchronous discussions." *Rural Special Education Quarterly,* 23(2), 33–36.

Hodges, C. B., and Cowan, S. F. (2012). "Preservice teachers' views of instructor presence in online courses." *Journal of Digital Learning in Teacher Education,* 28(4), 139–145.

Hou, J., and Wu, S. (2011). "Analyzing the social knowledge construction behavioral patterns of an online synchronous collaborative discussion instructional activity using an instant messaging tool: A case study." *Computers and Education*, 57, 1459–1468.

Hwang, K., and Yang, C. (2008). "A synchronous distance discussion procedure with reinforcement mechanism: Designed for elementary school students to achieve the attending and responding stages of the affective domain teaching goals within a class period." *Computers and Education*, 51, 1538–1552.

Im, Y., and Lee, O. (2003–2004). "Pedagogical implications of online discussion for preservice teacher training." *Journal of Research on Technology in Education*, 36(2), 155–170.

Lowes, S. (2007). "Professional development for online teachers." In C. Cavanaugh and R. Blomeyer (Eds.), *What Works in K–12 Online Learning* (pp. 161–178). Retrieved from www.iste.org/images/excerpts/K12OLL-excerpt.pdf.

Marchand, G. C., and Guierrez, A. P. (2012). "The role of emotion in the learning process: Comparisons between online and face-to-face learning settings." *Internet and Higher Education*, 15, 150–160.

Meyer, A. and Rose, D. H. (2005). "The future is in the margins: The role of technology and disability in educational reform." In D. H. Rose, A. Meyer and C. Hitchcock (Eds.), *The Universally Designed Classroom: Accessible Curriculum and Digital Technologies* (pp. 13–35). Cambridge, MA: Harvard Education Press.

Rose, D. H., Harbour, W. S., Johnston, C. S., Daley, S. G., and Abarbanell, L. (2006). "Universal design for learning in postsecondary education: Reflections on principles and their application." *Journal of Postsecondary Education and Disability*, 19(2), 17.

Tempelaar, D. T., Niculescu, A., Reinties, B., Gijselaers, W. H., and Giesbers, B. (2011). "How achievement emotions impact students' decisions for online learning, and what precedes those emotions." *Internet and Higher Education*, 15, 161–169.

Vasquez, E., Forbush, D. E., Mason, L. L., Lockwood, A. R., and Gleed, L. (2011). "Delivery and evaluation of synchronous online reading tutoring to students at-risk of reading failure." *Rural Special Education Quarterly*, 30(3), 16–26.

Vasquez, E. and Serianni, B. A. (2012). "Research and practice in distance education for K–12 students with disabilities." *Rural Special Education Quarterly* 31(4) 33–42.

6

Student Engagement in Online and Distance Learning

Monica L. Simonsen
Mary E. Morningstar
Jingrong Xie
UNIVERSITY OF KANSAS

We have all struggled at some point with engaging each individual student in our courses. Whether it is the subject, the environment, instructional method or other factors that influence student motivation, as instructors we believe it is our responsibility to engage all learners. It's even more critical to find ways to motivate learners in distance education classes since they rely on feeling motivated to open up their computers and interact with peers and instructors. This aspect of UDL, that of developing multiple ways for students to engage in and outside the virtual world, helps students remain challenged and enthusiastic in their online programs.

Student Engagement in Online and Distance Learning

Online and distance learning has become more prevalent and familiar within higher education. Online college programs and classes are growing in popularity with overall enrollment increasing, despite a recent drop in higher education enrollment (Allen, Seaman, Poulin, and Straut, 2016). Online learning is the most current approach to adult distance learning and thereby, expands educational opportunities for nontraditional and disenfranchised learners (Moore, Dickson-Deane, and Galyen, 2010), because it removes the limitations of time and place.

Studies show that online learning is more cost effective and convenient and provides opportunities for greater numbers of students to continue their education (Richardson and Swan, 2003). Most often, the roles of students and instructors are transformed, with the instructor serving as facilitator, and students becoming active learners. However, shifting active learning of students requires deliberately planning and supporting engagement so that students feel connected to their program, peers, and instructors. Many authors assert that learner engagement is a strong predictor of achievement and personal development (Oncu and Cakir, 2011). Research has linked student engagement in purposeful activities to desired outcomes such as academic achievement and persistence (Kuh, 2009).

Student engagement is defined as the effort learners devote to educational activities (Oncu and Cakir, 2011) and has been described as a multidimensional construct composed of three components: behaviors, emotions, and cognitions (Fredricks, Blumenfeld, and Paris, 2004; Lam, Wong, Yang, and Liu, 2012). Emotional engagement includes positive and negative reactions to educational experiences, coursework, classmates, and instructors. Cognitive engagement captures students' investment in the academic learning and is enhanced when student curiosity is stimulated. Behavioral engagement refers to students' actions that keep them on track in their coursework such as turning in assignments and participating in discussions (Kahu, 2013). How students assign meaning to their coursework and, ultimately, their level of academic achievement will depend largely on how well the course is designed to foster high levels of engagement. Technology can be utilized as a lever to promote student engagement in order to maximize the power of computers and information technology as a catalyst for student success in post-secondary education (Chen, Lambert, and Guidry, 2010).

A growing body of research suggests that the social, instructional, and organizational climate of schools influences both students' engagement and their academic achievement (Sutton and Nora, 2009). Schools must consider the degree to which students feel connected to their respective online program as well as the associated norms that define the group (e.g., high expectations for learning) can affect students' behavior, including engagement and motivation, academic achievement, and challenging behavior in online learning environment. One approach to ensuring active student engagement is to design and develop online and distance programs using Universal Design for Learning (UDL) (Katz, 2013). Based on the UDL framework, one principle, *multiple means of engagement*, has been referred to as the "why" of learning (Rose and Meyer, 2002). Research showed that emotions and feelings impact students' learning (Rose and Dalton, 2009).

The National Survey of Student Engagement (NSSE, Kuh, 2009), evaluates the quality of five benchmarks that align within a UDL framework: (a) level of academic challenge, (b) active and collaborative learning, (c) student-faculty interaction, (d) enriching educational experience, and (e) supportive student environments. Research has shown that technology may be positively correlated with student engagement (Chen et al., 2010). Results from the Community College Survey of Student Engagement (CCSSE) found that although students in online-only classes were less engaged than students in blended classes; this was likely attributed to the pedagogical choices of the online course. For example, the authors point out that the students in the online courses only minimally participated in active and collaborative learning experiences, with limited social and academic support from peers and instructors (Fisher, 2010). Thus, promoting active student engagement requires a focus on essential program-wide elements as well as the pedagogy and instruction of each course. This chapter will describe UDL strategies that can be used both at the program and course-level to foster behavioral, emotional, and cognitive engagement of online students.

Creating a Climate of Program Engagement

Despite the fact that online and distant students may work autonomously from different locations, they typically are part of a program leading to a certificate or degree. Therefore, program structures and supports are an essential element toward fostering student engagement. Several program structures will be described with examples of successful implementation using a UDL framework including: (a) using a cohort model, (b) setting expectations for active engagement, and (c) designing highly support advisement.

Cohort model. By design, the most successful online and distance programs create cohorts of students who then move through their coursework with a set group of classmates (Garrison and Arbaugh, 2007). By engaging with the same classmates across most courses, students get to know peers and can even form lasting relationships (Abrami, Bures, Borokhovski, and Tamim, 2011). They first meet their cohort during their orientation (online or in person) and for the most part, take coursework with their cohort. Students with established cohort relationships progress from simply getting to know each other to working collaboratively on academic tasks (Garrison and Arbaugh, 2007). Past research in online special education programs has indicated that connections with peers were among the most valuable parts of the online learning experience (Morningstar, Kim, and Clark, 2008).

Setting expectations. Students' expectations about engaging in online and distance learning provide a baseline reference point for students to form judgments about learning experiences. Clear policies and procedures are especially important for online students who are likely to interact with program information primarily in an asynchronous manner, with minimal real-time communication, and most often, not direct face-to-face engagement. The shift toward a predominantly technology-based learning is challenging for many adult learners who may not be comfortable with a range of online tools (Cercone, 2008). Providing clear guidelines about technology requirements while offering support to students can help make this positive.

Designing an orientation session can include identifying student efficacy toward online learning. Using a quiz format will help students identify comfort levels with certain technologies. Orientations provide students with opportunities to meet their peers, submit sample assignments, and learn about their program of study. In addition, a focus on setting expectations for how to be a successful online student occurs during orientation: (a) how and when to communicate with the instructors; (b) who to turn to for help with technology questions; (c) how much time is expected to work on coursework each week; and (d) expectations for synchronous "real time" meetings or group projects are just a few. Addressing frequently asked questions early and proactively will help to set clear expectations and avoid miscommunications.

Finally, across a specific program, it is important to scaffold opportunities to expand technology skills. This may mean purposefully introducing certain technology that will be consistently used throughout the program for: (a) accessing content (e.g., how to log onto online library, online learning modules, accessing interactive videos), and (b) acting and expressing learning (e.g., online discussion boards, VoiceThread, Zaption, Moodle, Padlet). This explicit instruction and support will help to accommodate the learner variability and enable students with varied experiences to access and participate in the course content.

Supportive Advisement. In addition to differences in technology skills, students in online and distance classes bring a variety of personal and professional experiences and goals to their coursework. Consistent, accessible advising is a principle component of any program to help ensure that students' career goals are being met and that coursework aligns are desired goals. Advisement structures may incorporate various levels of personalization, with the most successful having student advisement counselors in place who are able to consistently engage with students throughout their program; addressing program-level questions, and serving as a first point of contact for enrollment and other programmatic concerns. Counselors then work closely with course instructors, and particularly spend time intensively communicating with students not participating in classes. Faculty advisors and instructors are actively supporting student engagement both in classes as well as throughout the program. Having individualized, consistent, informed points of contact provides students with the guidance needed to stay on track and feel connected. Regardless of the structure and allocation of personnel, it is critical that the students can reach out to the right person with questions or concerns.

Universal Design of Courses for Active Engagement

Student engagement (social/emotional, behavioral, and cognitive) is largely dependent on the structure, design, content, and facilitation of the coursework. Despite the lack of face-to-face interactions, online and distance classes can offer relevant and rich opportunities for students to form meaningful connections. To ensure purposeful, motivated learners, carefully crafted approaches to stimulating interest and motivation is critical. For example, using case-based approaches to learning, and requiring learners apply content to real life professional or personal situations will increase engagement. Universally designing learning experiences so that students are connected with their peers and instructors, and are actively engaged will be discussed next.

Peer to peer interactions. Simply placing students into a class together is not sufficient for building a professional learning community; rather, the course must be designed to foster opportunities for meaningful, mutually beneficial interactions, including designing assignments that require students to co-construct knowledge through collaboration. Online discussion forums are commonly used in distance programs that must be designed to elicit student responds to both content-specific prompts, as well as to classmates' posts. The size of discussion groups, the nature of the question/discussion prompt, and the types of instructor facilitation have an impact on the level of engagement and quality of academic discourse (Kim, 2013; Hall, 2015). The following guidelines should be considered:

- Create small groups for student projects and discussion forums.
- Specify roles and responsibilities for group projects.

- Assign weekly discussion forum leaders (2–3 leaders per weekly discussion.)
- Provide frequent and meaningful instructor contributions to the discussion; prompting learners to think more deeply and with greater support from readings and other materials.
- Vary the types of discussion prompts to best elicit dynamic discussions (e.g., opinions, personal story, rebuttals, etc.) and avoid content-specific answers that do not allow students to continue to discuss.
- Utilize a grading rubric to provide specific feedback on participation (i.e., quality of posts, how often students respond to others, and timely postings.)

Recognizing the importance of providing opportunities for multiple means of expression will ensure students participate through more than text-based discussion. For example, have students create a video response to a question, or to share an assignment they completed for class. Student can then see and hear their classmates, making more tangible connections. Although most learning management system platforms have built in capabilities to utilize audio and/or video files, using outside tools (i.e., VoiceThread, www.voicethread.com) can expand opportunities specifically to foster seeing and hearing each other in asynchronous environments as well as responding to classmates through text, voice or video comments.

For real-time engagement, hosting a series of online video meetings can be highly effective. Real-time video meetings allow students to interact with the instructor, have questions immediately answered, and further deepen connections. Real-time meetings are particularly helpful at the beginning of a course to orient students to course expectations and requirements. Instructors can also customize communication strategies to incorporate online meetings and virtual office hours, particularly when major assignments are due.

One major appeal of online and distance learning is the flexibility it affords students to work when it best suits them during the day or evening. Courses should therefore design opportunities for students to asynchronously interact and learn from one another. A range of customized online tools can be used to allow students to co-construct knowledge without all being online at the same time. Most course management systems include blogs, wikis, and other tools for students to collaborate on group projects. Other online tools are highly beneficial, such as crafting a paper together or completing a scavenger hunt table using Google Docs https://www.google.com/docs/about/), or sharing articles and resources using Dropbox (www.Dropbox.com), or web resources using Padlet (www.Padlet.com). For students who are not extremely vocal or demonstrative in face-to-face courses, opportunities to work asynchronously may actually provide unique and improved collaboration with peers.

Engaging with instructors. In a traditional face-to-face course, instructors can talk about assignments and respond immediately to questions. In the online or distance classroom, students may rely on email to ask clarifying questions and maybe working on classwork when instructors are not as readily available (i.e., evenings, weekends). To foster meaningful content-related engagement among students, the course materials must be accessible and the directions and guidelines for all assignments must be clear. There are a variety of universally designed approaches to making course expectations explicit. For example, instructors should develop grading rubrics and provide specific constructive feedback both in writing and as video feedback segments. Instructors can create online announcements through most course management systems as a way to provide reminders of upcoming assignments, to check in with students, and to provide clarity of grading expectations.

Instructors can also showcase samples of quality assignments, describe specific course requirements, and provide tips to students. One strategy for doing this is to create a screen captured video (e.g., using Camtasia, Screencast-o-matic) of the assignment while the instructor explains about the major elements of the project. Using similar technology, instructors can narrate explicit feedback to students. This is particularly helpful when providing feedback on edited papers or major project assignments.

Project-based learning. Engagement is promoted through pedagogy requiring students to expend collaborative effort for solving problems (Meyer, 2014). Designing coursework that allows expression of learning and problem solving is most effective when considered as project-based (Van Rooij, 2009; Shea and Bidjerano, 2009). One strategy used to ensure students continue to progress toward satisfactory completion is to design a running project, where students, either individually or in small groups, scaffold success across multiple points in time with explicit instruction feedback at consecutive points in time. This approach has been found to be highly effective for ensuring students maintain high levels of engagement throughout the class, with opportunities for improvements and enhancements over time.

Similar to a running project, often at the end point of a program, students complete a culminating experience. For distance students, creating an online competency-based portfolio ensures ongoing development. Using this approach, students identify critical learning experiences from across their program as these align with identified program competencies. This approach can use a combination of the typical course management system for maintaining feedback and grading, along with online portfolio tools such as Wix (www.wix.com) and Weebly (www.weebly.com). Students can create a personalized portfolio, post reflections of learning, and identify critical competencies associated with products. Instructors provide seamless guidance and feedback using rubrics with regard to student attainment of essential competencies. Such a portfolio may also include videos of students applying learning to real life settings (e.g., in a classroom, on the job, etc.), and instructors provide coaching and feedback.

Summary

Well-designed distance and online programs and courses adhere to essential elements of UDL including: (a) clear goals, (b) planning for learner variability; (c) flexible methods and materials; and (d) timely progress monitoring (Nelson and Basham, 2014). Ensuring student engagement has been considered within the Community of Inquiry (COI) model (Shea and Bidjerano, 2009) which posits learning consists of three "presences:" teaching (i.e., well-designed and facilitated courses), social (i.e., learning interactions with peers and instructors), and cognitive (i.e., exploration and resolution of problems). In order to foster active engagement, identifying a range of learning modalities is more likely to appeal to a broader range of students who may come to the learning experience with varying prerequisite skills, learning styles, and reference points. Varying the ways students interact with the material, their classmates, and their instructors will foster a student experience that promotes active student engagement and improved student outcomes.

References

Allen, I. E., Seaman, J., Poulin, R., and Straut, T. T. (2016). *Tracking Online Education in the United States.* Babson Survey Research Group and Quahog Research Group, LLC. Retrieved on April 1, 2016 from http://onlinelearningsurvey.com/reports/onlinereportcard.pdf.

Abrami, P. C., Bernard, R. M., Bures, E. M., Borokhovski, E., and Tamim, R. M. (2011). "Interaction in distance education and online learning: Using evidence and theory to improve practice." *Journal of Computing in Higher Education, 23*(2–3), 82–103.

Cercone, K. (2008). "Characteristics of adult learners with implications for online learning design." *AACE Journal, 16*(2), 137–159.

Chen, P. S. D., Lambert, A. D., and Guidry, K. R. (2010). "Engaging online learners: The impact of Web-based learning technology on college student engagement." *Computers & Education, 54*(4), 1222–1232.

Fredericks, J. A., Blumenfeld, P. C., and Paris, A. H. (2004). "School engagement: Potential of the concept, state of the evidence." *Review of Educational Research, 74*(1), 59–109.

Garrison, D. R. and Arbaugh, J. B. (2007). "Researching the Community of Inquiry Framework: Review, issues, and future directions." *Internet and Higher Education, 10*, 157–172.

Hall, R. A. (2015). "Critical thinking in online discussion boards: Transforming an anomaly." *The Delta Kappa Gama Bulletin, 81*(3), 21–27.

Katz, J. (2013). "The three block model of universal design for learning (UDL): Engaging students in inclusive education." *Canadian Journal of Education, 36*(1), 153–194.

Kim, J. (2013). "Influence of group size on students' participation in online discussion forums." *Computers & Education, 62*, 123–129.

Kahu, E. R. (2013). "Framing student engagement in higher education." *Studies in Higher Education, 38*(5), 758–773.

Kuh, G. D. (2009). "The National Survey of Student Engagement: Conceptual and empirical foundations." *New Directions for Institutional Research*, (141), 5–20. DOI: 10.1002/ir.283.

Lam, S., Wong, B., Yang, H., and Liu, M. (2012). "Understanding Student Engagement with a Conceptual Model." In *Handbook of Research on Student Engagement*, edited by S. Christenson, A. Reschly, and C. Wylie, 403–420. Heidelberg: Springer.

Meyer, Katrina (2014). "Student Engagement Online: What Works and Why." *ASHE Higher Education Report, 40*(6).

Moore, J. L., Dickson-Deane, C., and Galyen, K. (2011). "E-learning, online learning, and distance learning environments: Are they the same?" *The Internet and Higher Education, 14*(2), 129–135.

Morningstar, M. E., Kim, K., and Clark, G. M. (2008). "Evaluating a transition personnel preparation program: Identifying transition competencies of practitioners." *Teacher Education and Special Education, 31*(1), 47–58.

Nelson, L. L. and Basham, J. D. (2014). "A blueprint for UDL: Considering the design of implementation." Lawrence, KS: UDL-IRN. Retrieved from http://udl-irn.org.

Oncu, S., and Cakir, H. (2011). "Research in online learning environments: Priorities and methodologies." *Computers & Education, 57*(1), 1098–1108.

Richardson, J. C., and Swan, K. (2003). "Examining social presence in online courses in relation to students' perceived learning and satisfaction." *The Journal of Asynchronous Learning Networks, 7*(1), 68–83.

Rose, D. H., and Dalton, B. (2009). "Learning to read in the digital age." *Mind, Brain, and Education, 3*(2), 74–83.

Rose, D. H., and Meyer, A. (2002). *Teaching Every Student in the Digital Age: Universal Design for Learning.* Association for Supervision and Curriculum Development, 1703 N. Beauregard St., Alexandria, VA 22311-1714 (Product no. 101042: $22.95 ASCD members; $26.95 nonmembers).

Shea, P., and Bidjerano, T. (2009). "Community of inquiry as a theoretical framework to foster 'epistemic engagement' and 'cognitive presence' in online education." *Computers & Education, 52*(3), 543–553.

Sutton, S. C. and Nora, A. (2008). "An exploration of college persistence for student enrolled in web-enhanced courses: A multivariate analytic approach." *Journal of College Student Retention: Research, Theory & Practice, 10*(1), 21–37.

Van Rooij, S. W. (2009). "Scaffolding project-based learning with the project management body of knowledge (PMBOK®)." *Computers & Education, 52*(1), 210–219.

7

Universal Design through Openly Networked Connected Learning

Laura Gogia
Jonathan Becker
VIRGINIA COMMONWEALTH UNIVERSITY

The purpose of the universal design for learning (UDL) framework is to support the development of flexible curricular and instructional approaches that provide all learners with the dispositions required to engage in fulfilling, strategic, and productive lifelong learning (National Center for Universal Design for Learning, 2014). As an emerging digital pedagogy that aims to promote inclusiveness, engagement, and deeper student learning, connected learning presents a compelling orientation consistent with and, arguably, advancing of UDL principles in online learning. At Virginia Commonwealth University (VCU), faculty are designing connected learning courses ("connected courses") in openly networked online spaces where students engage in course-related discourse, research, and writing with each other on the web. The combined qualities of connected, open, and networked instructional design have resulted in promising manifestations of personalized, reflective, and integrated learning. This chapter provides a brief introduction to connected learning in openly networked spaces as interpreted and implemented at VCU. We will use two connected course exemplars, *Thoughtvectors: Inquiry and the Craft of Argument* and *Collaborative Curiosity: Designing Community Engaged Research*, to demonstrate the overlap and connections between UDL and openly networked connected learning.

Introduction to Connected Learning

Inspired by Dewey, Montessori, and original ethnographic inquiry, the Digital Media Lab (DML) Research Hub published an agenda for connected learning research and instructional design in 2013 (Ito et al., 2013). Illustrated in **Figure 1**, the pedagogical framework presented in the agenda consists of three learning principles (interest-driven, peer culture, and academically oriented) and three design principles (shared purpose, production centered, and openly networked). The learning principles emphasize the diverse spaces in which youth learn, including their personal hobbies, extra- and co-curricular activities, and formal academic experiences. The design principles highlight strategies that instructors might use to create experiential, social, and digital learning experiences that help students make meaningful connections between personal passions and academic, professional, or civic-minded goals (Ito et al., 2013). Openly networked learning spaces are web-based environments in which students have access to and can interact with resources, audiences, and individuals "beyond the classroom," on the open, or "public," web. When students learn publicly, they are able to access resources, inspiration, collaborators, mentors, and audiences beyond the local academic community (Groom and Lamb, 2014).

At VCU, various faculty members have explored openly networked learning opportunities for the purpose of promoting educational inclusiveness and student engagement and success (VCU Office of the Provost and Vice President for Academic Affairs, 2014). To help facilitate these opportunities, VCU established an open, networked campus publishing platform named after the university mascot ("RamPages;" http://rampages.us). When VCU faculty, staff, and students create RamPage sites to support their personal learning, social and co-curricular activities, and formal academic courses and scholarship, the content becomes networked to form a rich, virtual learning community layered onto and extending beyond the physical VCU campus.

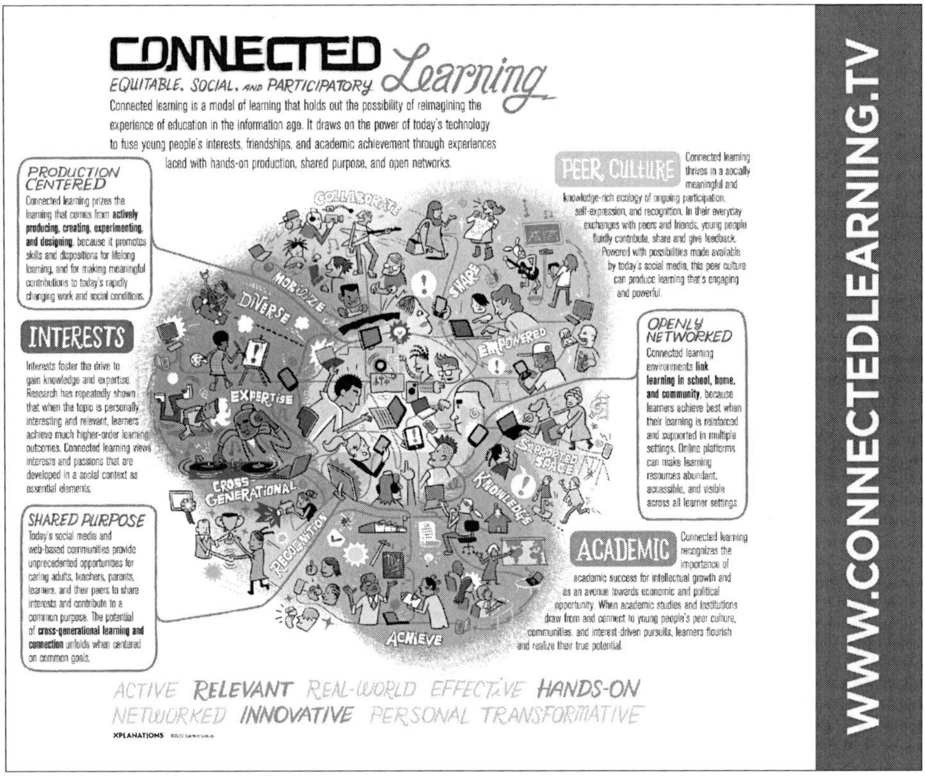

Figure 7.1: Connected Learning Framework Infographic. Developed and licensed under 4.0 BY-SA CC License by Connected Learning Research Network and Digital Media and Learning Research Hub.

Connected Courses

Since its inception in 2014, RamPages has expanded to more than 16,000 sites in the first two years and continues to grow rapidly. Increasingly, the platform is being used across a variety of disciplines and programs to support formal, academic credit-bearing "connected courses." Although each connected course is different, they share an underlying course structure: (1) a majority, if not all, course materials, activities, and group announcements are found on a public course website; (2) students complete at least some of their assignments as public blog posts on their personal websites (while many students choose to start a RamPages website, some use other blogging platforms); (3) students' blog posts are aggregated by an RSS feed to the course website so that all blogged assignments can be viewed in one space (known as the course "bloggregate"); and (4) students participate in course-related public discourse, such as commenting on each other's blog posts and/or engaging in conversation on social media platforms like Twitter. Thoughtvectors and Collaborative Curiosity are two examples of connected courses offered at VCU between 2014 and 2015.

Thoughtvectors. *UNIV 200: Inquiry and the Craft of Argument,* better known as "Thoughtvectors," was the first connected course piloted at VCU in the summer of 2014. It was a fully-online variant of a research writing course taken by all VCU undergraduates as part of the first of three tiers of the general education curriculum. The term, "Thoughtvectors," refers to Doug Engelbart's conceptualization of "thought vectors in concept space," the mental environment or integrated domain afforded by personal, interactive, networked computing. Students engaged in reading, blogging, tweeting, commenting, collaborating, and creating around the works of Internet pioneers and, in some cases, the Internet pioneers themselves (through the use of open video conferencing platforms and arranged interviews). Ninety-five VCU undergraduates were formally enrolled across six sections of the course. Over 500 "open participants" (i.e. learners who do not pay for coursework and do not receive formal instructor feedback or academic credit) also engaged in at least some of the Thoughtvectors course activities. **Figure 2** provides further description of the Thoughtvectors learning space. Students created their own websites, which were networked together through RSS feeds at the levels of their designated section ("clubhouses") and the main course website (Thoughtvectors.net). By aggregating student, faculty, and open participant work at the level of the main course website, students could see, comment on, and connect across all six sections and to the open participants beyond the classroom. Common tags for assignments across all sections allowed students to hone in on particular work products.

Collaborative Curiosity. Thoughtvectors was followed by a number of variations on the connected course theme, including *Collaborative Curiosity: Designing Community Engaged Research* (CMST 691). This eight-week, fully-online graduate course was offered to open participants and academic credit-bearing students as an introduction to the purpose, design, and practice of community engaged research. Eleven VCU graduate students formally registered and earned credit for the course, but approximately fifteen additional open (unenrolled, non-credit earning) participants also engaged in and contributed to the course in recognizable, meaningful, or consistent capacities. Each week, participants engaged with community research experts via open video conferencing platforms; participated in synchronous, Twitter-based discussions of assigned readings; wrote community engaged research proposals in a series of blog posts; blogged reflectively on differences between community engaged research and other forms of research; and created digital "makes" around important questions in community engaged research. Collaborative Curiosity differed from Thoughtvectors in that it consisted of only one section, so while students created and used their own websites, only one layer of networking occurred at the level of the main course website.

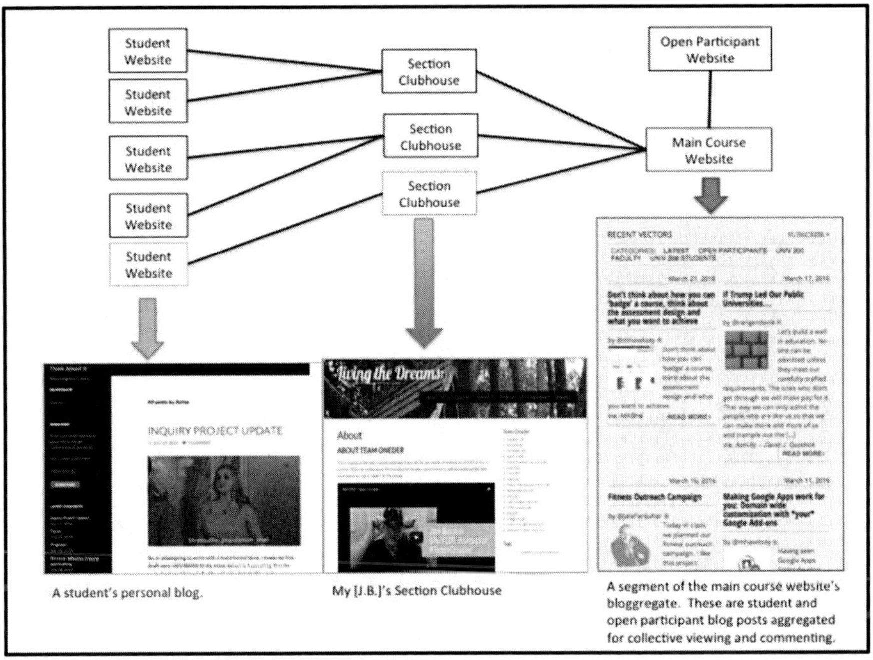

Figure 7.2: Thoughtvectors Learning Space

The "Why" of Learning: Permission to Wonder and Wander

The UDL and connected learning frameworks draw from existing educational research to argue that students who understand the "why" of their learning are most likely to achieve their goals (Kumpulainen and Sefton-Green, 2014; National Center for Universal Design for Learning, 2014). Student perceptions of agency, belongingness, and academic relevance are all associated with student engagement (Osterman, 2000). Even as the Thoughtvectors and Curious Collaboration instructors worked to create a strong social and teaching presence to provide appropriate scaffolding and safe spaces, the openly networked structure of the courses gave students the permission to wander: to explore, experiment, and focus on resources and areas of content that were interesting and relevant to them as individuals. This section explores how the elements of connected learning found in Thoughtvectors and Collaborative Curiosity also fulfilled UDL criteria related to the "why of learning" and resulted in uniquely rich manifestations of deeper and integrative learning among the students.

Agency. The UDL framework for learning advocates for designs that "optimize individual choice and autonomy" for the purpose of recruiting student interest (National Center for Universal Design for Learning, 2014). For every VCU connected course, including Thoughtvectors and Collaborative Curiosity, students are provided with the opportunity to create, style, and manage their own website. While they are free to use any blogging platform desired, they are encouraged to use RamPages because of the additional content and technical support made available through the university. The advantages of student ownership over their blog spaces is multifold. First, students often find the opportunity to style and structure their own online learning spaces (rather than being limited by a templated or "one-size-fits-all" space) to be more engaging (Yancey, 2009). Second, the shift from institutional to student ownership encourages students to use their blog spaces in interdisciplinary, cross-contextual (i.e., extracurricular, co-curricular, and formal academic) ways that fall outside the traditional purview of academic coursework (Downes, 2007). Finally, students can access their learning products beyond the academic calendar and their course of study and share them with the external stakeholders of their choice. For example, one student chose to use a Tumblr site for the Thoughtvectors course because she was familiar and comfortable with that platform. Furthermore, her Tumblr site reflects her aesthetic sensibilities, including the addition of a music widget that plays some of her favorite songs for visitors to the site. This feeling of working in a comfortable, personalized space gives students a feeling of agency and ownership of their learning space.

Academic Relevance. Several aspects of the UDL framework touch on the importance of academic relevance, in terms of recruiting student interest and "heightening the salience of goals and objectives" to promote purposeful learning (National Center for Universal Design for Learning, 2014). These overlap with the connected learning principle of interest-driven learning, through which students are offered as much freedom as possible to adapt course objectives, activities, and content to meet their personal learning interests and goals. Thoughtvectors and Curious Collaboration students chose the topics of their major projects. In both cases, many students focused on their major area of study or research. For example, in Thoughtvectors, a student enrolled in the pre-health program completed her final project on the Affordable Care Act, while an engineering major focused on reforming STEM education. Similarly, final projects in Collaborative Curiosity mirrored students' fields of primary research, from autism research to social services for hispanic communities.

Additionally, the Thoughtvectors course had a purposeful meta layer to it. All sections of UNIV200 at VCU are titled, "Inquiry and the Craft of Argument." The special digital engagement primer had a nickname (Thoughtvectors) as well as an alternate title: "Living the Dreams: Digital Investigation and Unfettered Minds." This alternate title hinted at the idea that the course would explore what it means to do inquiry at a time when the visions of new media pioneers had largely come to fruition. Reading the original works of new media pioneers such as Doug Engelbart, Vannevar Bush, Alan Kay, Adele Goldberg, and others may seem atypical for a course about research writing. However, reading about Bush's idea of the Memex and Kay and Goldberg's work on the Dynabook, for example, cause the students to reflect on the history and the ideas behind the very digital tools they are using to conduct digital investigations. This effort towards metacognition is valuable in and of itself, but the instructors also try to make this meta layer explicit as a means of heightening the salience of the goals and objectives of the course. Further heightening the salience of the goals and objectives is the explicit lesson that these methods of digital investigation are integrative and relevant to what remains of the academic journey for undergraduates.

Community. Although openly networked learning spaces allow students access to a public stage for their ideas and aspirations, connected learning values the learning community, or environments in which participants build trust, feel safe to be honest and take risks, and co-create knowledge with peers and mentors. The concept of "presence," especially teaching presence, plays a large role in the development, sustainability, and effectiveness of learning communities (Garrison, Anderson, and Archer, 2010). In openly networked learning spaces, teaching presence often involves modelling and actively collaborating with students to define, curate, and produce course content (Anderson and Dron, 2010). To jumpstart their teaching presence in this eight-week course, instructors from both courses filmed course trailers, designed specifically to spotlight the instructors and their personalities as much as the course content and format. Before and during the course, instructors engaged in reflective blogging, which was aggregated along with student work on the course website. They commented on student blog posts and engaged participants on Twitter during and between scheduled discussions. Instructors from both courses also recruited members of their personal and professional learning networks to intermingle, support, and act as mentors for the students in the learning communities.

Working in openly networked communities provides opportunities for serendipitous meetings and collaborations between participants that would not occur in more traditional, closed settings. This manifests itself in a variety of ways. For example, two Thoughtvectors students registered in different sections of the course opted to collaborate on their final inquiry project, crafting both sides of an argument in the form of a multimodal, web-based composition. Additionally, one student was working on an inquiry project about math education in the K–12 system. A VCU faculty member, not one of the assigned instructors, shared a link to one of the student's blog posts on Twitter where it was seen by the executive director of a statewide educational technology organization. She commented on the student's post, giving the student perspective from an expert and a member of the larger community already in conversation with some of the ideas with which the student was wrestling in the blog post. Had the student not been given permission to wonder out loud, that connection to the community would not have been made.

The "What" of Learning: Making and Visualizing Connections

UDL encourages educators to emphasize "patterns, critical features, big ideas, and relationships" across contexts as a means to increase the likelihood of comprehension and knowledge transfer across more students (National Center for Universal Design for Learning, 2014). It encourages active learning techniques in which students are required to process, visualize, and manipulate information. Similarly, connected learning asserts the value of connectivity, or the deeper learning that occurs when students form, document, and reflect on meaningful connections across concepts, people, contexts, and time (Kumpulainen and Seton-Green, 2014). Learning through connection is a multistep, experiential process by which students experience or form connections, reflect on them, critique and analyze them, and experiment with new connections that move them forward towards their learning goals. There are many ways to facilitate connectivity. When students add hyperlinks or engage other individuals on digital platforms, that activity is automatically captured and stored by the platform in ways that are retrievable and visualizable. These "digital traces" become descriptions, which, when reconstructed appropriately, flesh out relationships or connections formed through digital networks. Digital scholars argue that act of tracing stimulates self-reflection and pattern recognition; establishes a tangible product for mutual consideration and planning; and documents interaction so that it becomes an account, story, or explanation of process (Rice, 2011). We offer hyperlinks and network analysis as two powerful examples of how digital spaces can facilitate the documentation, visualization, and student reflection on patterns, relationships, and their own performance within the course.

Hyperlinks. Specific to online spaces, hyperlinks allow web-based authors to connect specific locations within their websites or posts (typically a word, phrase, or image) to another web document. When the hyperlink is clicked, the reader is automatically transported to the second web document, either in the same or a different web browser window. The incorporation of a hyperlink into a web document offers the opportunity to provide additional information (Gao, Li, and Zhang, 2012) and greater flexibility in ordering and reordering web-based content (Yancey, 2004).

Though not impossible, creating a sense of community purely within a learning management system (LMS) requires a considerable amount of work by the instructor. In a connected learning paradigm, however, where students learn out loud and publish their thinking and work to blogs, the seemingly simple technology of hypertext automatically puts student work in conversation and in community with other student work.

> . . . a blog functions as an amalgam of document and person, and blogs link hypertext networks with social networks. In addition, people can comment on blogs, thereby creating an explicit link from themselves to the blog. By treating people as synonymous with the blogs that they author, comments that people make on each other's blogs may then be viewed as reciprocal links in a social network. The patterns of interconnections between large numbers of blogs thus forms a social hypertext, and this social hypertext not only conveys hyperlinked information, but also may create forms of virtual community as people establish online presences and locales, and communicate with each other, through webs of interconnected blogs (Chin and Chignell, 2006, p. 11).

In Thoughtvectors, students were explicitly asked to link to other student posts throughout the semester. That is, they were asked to show how their work was part of a community of scholars though the simple act of hyperlinking. In Collaborative Curiosity, students tended to use hyperlinks to provide reference or source information, greater detail or definition, illustration, or contextualizing information related to their personal experience. Research performed at the time of the course suggested that student use of hyperlinks could be easily categorized and visualized to support concrete conversations with students on how they were forming connections between information sources, content, and their thoughts within and extending beyond the context of the course (Gogia, 2016).

Table 7.1: Examples of Hyperlink Usage in Student Blogs (Gogia, 2016)

BLOG POST EXCERPT*	HYPERLINKED WORD or EMBEDDED MATERIAL	HYPERLINK/EMBEDDED MATERIAL TYPE & SOURCE	TYPE OF CONNECTION
Smith (2010) suggests that verbal and nonverbal communication can lead to increased...	Smith(2010)	Journal article	Citation
	Nonverbal	Slides published on a digital slide sharing platform	Description
If you would like more information on this topic, check out what these organizations have to say: National Institutes of Health	National Institutes of Health	Government-sponsored webpage designed for public consumption of research	Additional Resources
...this could be done Mad Libs style.	Mad Libs	MadLibs webpage	Description
Phenomenology would be one appropriate research approach. It has been used in similar studies in the nursing and allied health fields (Howard & Jeffries, 2014).	Phenomenology	Stanford Encyclopedia of Philosophy entry on phenomenology	Description
	Howard & Jeffries, 2014	Journal article	Citation
In last week's post, I proposed a list of questions that are meant to inspire my research for this course. This week...	Post	Previous post	Personal context
I am exploring this topic as part of this course..."	Course	Course website	Course context
Barn raisings, still common in parts of the country, demonstrate the benefits of community by...In the picture....		Embedded image credited to a Wikipedia article (public domain)[b]	Illustration
Additional Questions		Embedded image with unknown source	Aesthetics

[a] These excerpts are modeled after samples from learner blog posts. Exact phrasing was changed to protect the privacy of the original authors.
[b] Photo attributed to Alexander W. Galbraith, via Wikimedia Commons. Retrieved from: https://commons.wikimedia.org/wiki/File%3ABarn_raising_in_Lansing.jpg

Network Analysis. Easily accessible through open source software and geared to novices and experts alike, network analysis generates graphs to describe the nodes (objects or people) and the edges (ties, interactions, or relationships) that make up a network (Wasserman and Faust, 1994). They can be viewed and interpreted in dynamic, real time or as static points in time. Network analysis was used in Thoughtvectors and Collaborative Curiosity to illustrate the Twitter-based social interactions between students, instructors, and other participants. Instructors in both courses encouraged students to diversity their patterns of social interaction, so that they might benefit from the variety of each others past experiences and perspectives. The network analyses were used to capture and reflect back social interaction to the students, so that they could use the information to consider and assess their own patterns of participation.

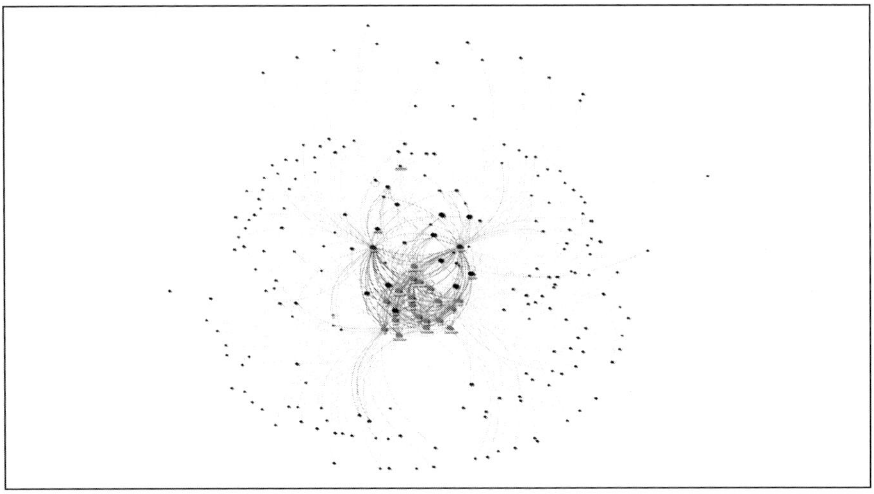

Figure 7.3: Sociogram of Collaborative Curiosity Twitter activity, created through a social network analysis of all tweets containing the course hashtag. The circles (or "nodes") represent individual course participants and have been de-identified for the purposes of this publication. The lines ("edges") between nodes represent tweeted interactions between participants. Instructors used sociograms such as these to reflect participation patterns back to the students, so that they could reflect on, evaluate, and potentially change their behavior.

The "How" of Learning: Incorporating Multimodal Expression

The UDL framework recommends the encouragement of multimodal expression as a means of enabling students to deepen and diversify their approaches to course material. One of the six fundamental design principles of connected learning is "production-centered," reminding educators to design learning experiences that allow students to learn through making things that are concrete and meaningful to them. When UDL and connected learning are combined in digital environments, digital makes (a.k.a. creative makes, daily creates, or daily makes) emerge as a means to help students sharpen digital literacies, foster creativity, and manifest concrete connections across contexts, concepts, space, and time.

Digital makes. Digital makes are short (designed to last 15–20 minutes), frequent assignments (daily or weekly) that help students practice multimodal expressivity while also enhancing their digital technical skills and engaging them with course concepts. Digital makes are typically aggregated and posted on the web for others to consider, be inspired by, and comment on. The graduate students enrolled in Collaborative

Curiosity were asked to find or create images and videos to help them reflect on some of the more abstract concepts found in the course. The students embedded the image or video into a blog post and briefly explained their creative choice in terms of the assigned prompt. In the case of the first prompt, "What does community mean to you?" one student embedded a photograph of a quilt and described how it acted as a metaphor for community as the blending of disparate parts to make a whole. Another used a graphic design application to combine a personal photograph and a favorite quotation to embody her definition of community. However, many students chose pictures of geographic-bounded locations, triggering them to uncover and then explore their limited conceptualizations of community.

Multimodal projects. In Thoughtvectors, multimodality played a large role in the final project of the course. Students are asked to work throughout the semester towards the completion of an inquiry project. That project involves crafting an argument on a topic of the students' choice based on research students do throughout the course. The arguments are published on a web-based platform of the students' choosing. Some students choose to stay within the university-supported Web publishing platform, RamPages, but many others select alternate platforms including Tumblr, Medium, Weebly, and Wix. Additionally, students are strongly encouraged to consider what publishing to the Web allows and what the multimodality afforded by Web publishing brings to bear on the argument as crafted. Selfe (2009) argues that writing instructors need to understand "composition as a multimodal rhetorical activity. As an implicit nod to the UDL framework, Selfe goes on to write that we need to "provide students the opportunities of developing expertise with all available means of persuasion and expression, so that they can function as literate citizens in a world where communications cross geopolitical, cultural, and linguistic borders and are enriched rather than diminished by semiotic dimensionality" (618).

> When we insist on print as the primary, and most formally acceptable, modality for composing knowledge, we usurp these rights and responsibilities on several important intellectual and social dimensions, and, unwittingly, limit students' sense of rhetorical agency to the bandwidth of our own interests and imaginations (618).

One student, writing on Medium.com about "Mommy Wars" online, was able to incorporate an image that she composed consisting of various headlines from around the Web about the so-called "Mommy Wars."

This image worked in support of the claim early in the argument that the "Mommy Wars" are a real and ubiquitous phenomenon. Another student asserted agency over the composition by choosing a theme that established an aesthetic of darkness in support of an argument about the long-term effects of nuclear bombs on Hiroshima.

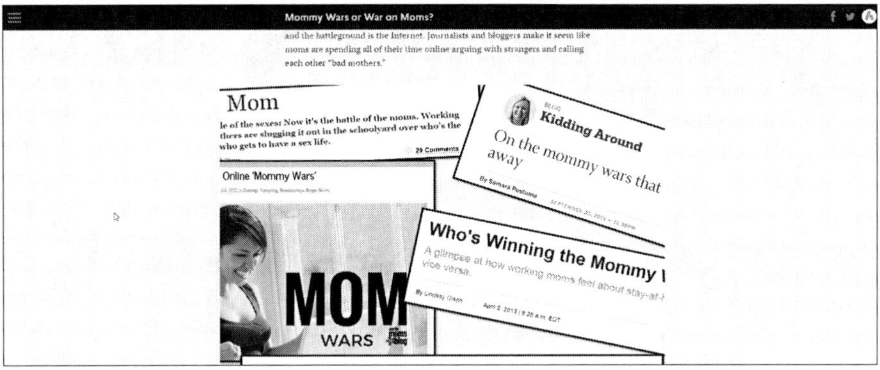

Figure 7.4: Mommy Wars.

Figure 7.5: Examples of multimodal, web-based projects created by students enrolled in Thoughtvectors.

Conclusion

Multimodal composition as a learning process and/or artifact is not limited to courses framed in a connected learning orientation, but it is only possible when students are allowed to work in openly networked spaces. This is true of the digital makes and it is only in openly networked spaces and platforms that hyperlinking is possible. Similarly, producing learning artifacts in openly networked spaces affords students the opportunity to connect their work to the greater community of people and ideas, thereby facilitating greater capacity to identify patterns, critical features, big ideas, and relationships. In other words, the connected learning design principles of production-centered and openly-networked are what allow students to engage in multimodal expression and composing in hypertext as a means of deeper and more diverse approaches to course material and activities. Thus, these design principles are not just consistent with key principles of universal design for learning, they actually advance those goals and objectives.

Connected learning as an orientation to online learning within formal academic settings is relatively new, even if it does build upon the work of longstanding theories of learning including social constructivism and constructionism. For some, it is overly complicated and some worry about what happens when connected learning gets used in formal educational settings.

> In short, the promise of connected learning is considerable. But, it is at risk of being "curricularised," of serving the cause of social reproduction more than that of social justice, and of being co-opted by corporate interests and institutional surveillance in ways that may lead students to resist rather than participate (Livingstone, 2016).

Those concerns notwithstanding, a (perhaps overly) simplistic way to think about connected learning is that it lives at the intersection of student-centered learning and the affordances of the modern Web. That is, the existence of the modern Web and the growth of the participatory culture around the Web mean there has never been a better time to be a learner. And, for educators, there has never been a better time to design online learning experiences that are consistent with the principles of universal design for learning.

References

Anderson, T., and Dron, J. (2010). "Three generations of distance education pedagogy." *The International Review of Research in Open and Distributed Learning*, 12(3), 80–97. DOI: http://dx.doi.org/10.19173/irrodl.v12i3.890.

Chin, A., and Chignell, M. (2006). "A social hypertext model for finding community in blogs." In Wiil, U. K., Nurnberg, P. J., and Rubart, J. (Eds.), (pp. 11–22) *Seventeenth ACM Conference on Hypertext and Hypermedia*. ACM Press: Odense, Denmark.

Downes, S. (2007). "Learning networks in practice." In D. Ley (Ed.), *Emerging Technologies for Learning*. National Research Council of Canada. Retrieved from: https://www.academia.edu/2869500/Learning_networks_in_practice.

Gao, D., Li, W., and Zhang, R. (2012). "Beyond Twitter text: A preliminary study on Twitter hyperlink and its application." In *Proceedings of International Conference on Computational Linguistics, Demonstration Papers* (pp. 155–162).

Garrison, D. R., Anderson, T., and Archer, W. (2010). "The first decade of the community of inquiry framework: A retrospective." *The Internet and Higher Education*, 13(1), 5–9.

Gogia, L. (2016). "Documenting student connectivity and use of digital annotation devices in Virginia Commonwealth University connected courses: An assessment toolkit for digital pedagogies in higher education." Retrieved from scholarscompass.vcu.edu/etd/4307.

Groom, J., and Lamb, B. (2014). "Reclaiming innovation." *Educause Review*, 49(3). Retrieved from: http://www.educause.edu/visuals/shared/er/extras/2014/ReclaimingInnovation/default.html.

Ito, M., Gutiérrez, K., Livingstone, S., Penuel, B., Rhodes, J., Salen, K., Schor, J., Sefton-Green, J., and Watkins, C. (2013). "Connected learning: An agenda for research and design." Irvine, CA: *Digital Media and Learning Research Hub*. Retrieved from: http://dmlhub.net/publications/connected-learning-agenda-for-research-and-design/.

Kumpulainen, K., and Sefton-Green, J. (2014). "What is connected learning and how to research it?" *International Journal of Learning and Media*, 4(2), 7–18. doi: 10.1162/IJLM_a_00091.

Livingstone, S. (2016, May 5). "Meet 'The Class.'" [Web log post]. Retrieved from http://dmlcentral.net/meet-the-class/.

National Center for Universal Design for Learning. (2014). "Universal Design for Learning Guidelines." Retrieved from: http://www.udlcenter.org/aboutudl/udlguidelines_theorypractice.

Osterman, K. F. (2000). "Students' need for belonging in the school community." *Review of Educational Research*, 70(3), 323–367.

Rice, J. (2011). "Networked assessment." *Computers and Composition*, 28, 28–29. doi:10.1016/j.compcom.2010.09.007.

Selfe, C. L. (2009). "The movement of air, the breath of meaning: Aurality and multimodal composing." *CCC*, 60(4): 616–663.

VCU Office of the Provost and Vice President for Academic Affairs (2014). "VCU Quality Enhancement Plan: Overview." Retrieved from: http://sacs.vcu.edu/quality-enhancementplan/.

Yancey, K. B. (2004). "Looking for sources of coherence in a fragmented world: Notes toward a new assessment design." *Computers and Composition*, 21(1), 89-102. doi:10.1016/j.compcom.2003.08.024.

Wasserman, S., and Faust, K. (1994). *Social Network Analysis: Methods and Applications*. Cambridge, UK: Cambridge University Press.

Yancey, K. B. (2009). "Electronic portfolios a decade into the twenty-first century: What we know, what we need to know." *Peer Review*, 11(1), 28.

8

Template for Universal Design for Learning Distance Education Courses

LaRon A. Scott
Peter Temple
Colleen A. Thoma
VIRGINIA COMMONWEALTH UNIVERSITY

One of the primary components of teaching and learning in distance education is the ability to create learning environments that are engaging, motivating, and provide access to contributors who share similar learning objectives (Salmon, 2002). For special education teachers, creating an online learning environment or course that is designed to consider the nuances of special education pedagogy has the opportunity to positively influence their preparation in distance education programs. As director of an online distance education master's program, I was convinced that it was necessary for our program to consider design, layout, curriculum, and other tools when we were planning to covert our face-to-face program online. This is where the idea of the UDL framework as a guide to enhance online coursework developed. In researching and reviewing course designs for converting our master's program to online, we found very little support for crafting our online program that would consider the specialized content, design, delivery, and type of impact we hoped to have on our distance education students. With the UDL framework as a guide, we sought to design courses and deliver coursework in our program so that teaching and learning opportunities met the needs of both students and faculty. As a result of our findings, we believed that it was necessary to share the design and delivery of our course development process.

This chapter has been arranged as a vehicle to showcase how we organized the merge of the UDL framework into our online courses. We have systematically outlined the stages that we used to develop our online courses utilizing the UDL framework. The four stages are organized throughout the chapter: design, architect, review, and implementation.

Terminology

Throughout this chapter, specific terms are used to define the roles of individuals and processes involved in online coursework development. **Table 8.1** features a guide to commonly used terminology. Your institution might not use the exact same terms, but the roles are largely universal.

Table 8.1: Terminology

Instructor	The individual(s) principally response for teaching the course, interacting with students, conducting grading and assessments, and monitoring student performance.
Program Management	The individual(s) responsible for administration and oversight of the online program(s).
Technologist	The principal individual(s) responsible for technology consulting and support, course design, development, implementation, and technical evaluation to enhance learning.
Course Developer	Individual(s) whom assist the technologist with course design, development, and implementation.
Widget	A web part, also called a widget or gadget, is a tool or script embedded on a webpage allowing specific content or media to be displayed (Dey, Abowd, and Salber, 2000). Web parts allow user interaction with media and content on the webpage by allowing cross-application communication.
Learning Management Systems (LMS)	A software application or combination of applications for the administration, documentation, tracking, reporting and delivery of electronic educational courses (Watson and Watson, 2007).
Digital Inclusion	The ability of individuals and groups to access and use information and communication technologies (Becker, et al., 2012).
Information Accessibility	A concept which ensures users of information systems possess the greatest opportunity and variety of methods to access information on a given platform or device (Teo, Chan, Wei, and Zhang, 2003).

Overview of the Process: Design, Architect, Review, and Implementation

Development and implementation of a UDL distance education program followed a specific process: design, architecture, review, and implementation. **Figure 1**, shown below, outlines the process and each of its four steps. During design, the instructor plans and develops the course to include goals, assessments, and learning objects, culminating in a course template. The instructor will also meet with the technologist to settle on which technologies would suit the needs of the course. From there, the technologist will take the template and begin to translate the course content into a specific online platform. The review phase is centered on two foci: digital inclusion and information accessibility. Digital inclusion is the ability of individuals and groups to access and utilize information and communication technologies (Becker, et al., 2012). Additionally, information accessibility is the concept which ensures users of information systems possess the greatest opportunity as well as have access to a variety of methods to access information on a given platform (the type of media utilized) or device (the actual tool by way they interact with the information, like a computer or tablet) (Teo, Chan, Wei, and Zhang, 2003). Implementation, the final step, happens when program management approves the course and students actively enroll into and participate in the online learning environment.

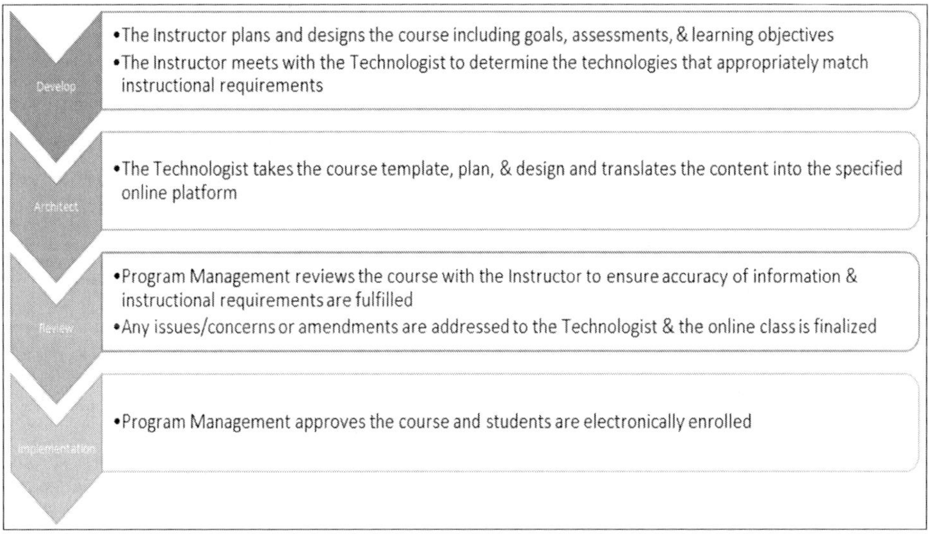

Figure 8.1: Process

Stage 1—Develop

Instructors and course developers should design courses with certain content in mind. These contents will also be explained in detail via the course platform to the students. The content is typically the subject meant for learning. Content is distributed in a course is through subcategories: course overview and introduction; learning objectives or competencies; assessment and measurement; instructional materials and course literature; course activities and student interaction; course technology, student support; and accessibility and usability (Quality Matters, 2014). These subcategories are recognized generally by the online and education communities as being the target goals for online program development (CEC, 2012; Green et al., 2005; McLaughlin and Lee, 2008). These subcategories are often considered when framing content for a course syllabus. It is essential that content dictates the initial phase of building an online course (Murray, 1998) as this is aligned with keeping online courses learner centered and with the guidelines of UDL (CAST, 2008; 2011).

Content

Content development (determining and creating the curriculum, text, images, videos, and other media) must start before course construction. When we first began the design of our online courses, we needed to figure out what exactly we wanted to teach. We chose not to simply transfer content from the face-to-face syllabus to the online format, because previous failures indicated that special education courses online required a stronger sense of pedagogy and a more concentrated effort to plan design and deliver. So, in our case, it was necessary to consider the content and pedagogy associated with the special education content. This focus led us to carefully analyze the special education teacher preparation guidelines for the Council for Exceptional Children (CEC). The CEC is the largest professional organization dedicated to improving the educational success of individuals with disabilities (CEC, 2015). For other programs with similar or dissimilar content focus, a beginning could be a professional organization, federal, or state drivers of *what to teach*.

Equally important when considering the content is an emphasis on learner-focused online education. This emphasis repeats in multiple special education and online pedagogies (CAST, 2008; CAST 2011; CEC, 2015; Green et al., 2005; McLaughlin and Lee, 2008). This importance is paramount in the CEC's guidelines for professional standards, listing learner development and the learning environment as its first principle (2015). Ultimately, an online course distributes content to learners. Therefore, it is important to consider what the learner's needs are when developing content. Students come from various backgrounds and will have different ways of absorbing the material. Some students are visual learners, finding videos and podcasts the best way to learn the lessons; others may find rote memorization or more traditional-style lectures more acclimating. When developing the content, it is important to keep your potential learners' needs in mind when determining what will work best conveying the lessons. **Table 8.2** includes examples of content formats. While this is by no means exhaustive, it can work as a starting point when determining what types of content you will implement into your online course.

Table 8.2: Content Format Examples

Textbooks	Textbooks assigned as part of the course literature; could be from a major publisher or independent publisher, in hard or soft back. Some publishers also offer online access and rentals to the texts.
Articles	Additional literature found online associated to the course or topic(s), such as journal articles, blog posts, or news sources.
Videos	A recording of moving visual images made digitally or on videotape, distributable via such services as YouTube, Vimeo, and Livestream.
Animations	A technique where successive drawings or models to create an illusion of movement when shown sequentially. Can be made and shared with Voki, Adobe Captivate.
PowerPoint Slides	A software package designed to create electronic presentations consisting of a series of separate pages or slides. Designed by Microsoft, but may also refer to Google Slides.
Podcasts	A digital audio file made available on the Internet for downloading to a computer or portable media player. Can use .mp3 files which are universal and work on many devices.
Discussion Boards	An Internet site where people can post and read messages, usually on a specific topic or area of interest. Should be directed for the course, and can be created within the platform.

The content outlined by the instructor will later dictate the technologies, formats, and techniques used. Traditional communication formats (ex. lectures) are not beneficial in online learning environments: thus, educators must use multimedia communication formats to deliver their lessons. Content development can be derived from many already existing sources: university/school guidelines or bulletins, course descriptions, current or previous syllabi, or the assigned textbook and course literature.

Platform Design and Navigation

Learning management systems (LMS) are a key component of online instruction as they are usually the platform on which the program is built (Benson and Palaskas, 2006; Conde et al., 2014). A LMS is a software application or combination of applications for the administration, documentation, tracking, reporting and delivery of electronic educational courses (Benson and Palaskas, 2006; Watson and Watson, 2007). LMSs are the foundation on which course developers construct online courses (Watson and Watson, 2007). Notable and widely-used platforms include Blackboard (2016), Edmodo (2016), Google Apps for Education (2016), and WordPress (2016). Deciding on the LMS requires attentive and careful consideration: many differ in the services, features, and functionality they offer (Watson and Watson, 2007). Course developers may benefit from testing several systems to determine which platform best suits program needs before final implementation.

Stage 2—Architect

Assembly of the online course should begin as stage 1 comes to an end. As mentioned earlier, creating the content is essential before design. Also important to consider when designing your course are the policies in place on smaller and grandiose scales. Policies, from within your organization to countrywide in scale, can largely affect how you present your course. There are industry standards and professional standards (CEC, 2015), federal and state laws (ADA, 1990; IDEA, 2004), and possibly university or school district policies which may guide your choice of platform, course design, and implementation. It is essential to familiarize yourself with the policies in place, as they may dictate how your course is structured.

UDL and Display of Content

We have emphasized the importance of UDL earlier in the development phase, and this is equally so in the architect stage. Consider the principle of Multiple Means of Representation (MMoR). This is broken down into three guidelines: provide options for perception, provide options for language and symbols, and provide options for comprehension (CAST, 2011).

Under providing options for perception, one must consider how information displays on the site. While you can provide options that customize the display of information, the design must remain consistent across the platform. Fonts, text size and color, use of media and images, phraseology, and language must be consistent throughout the entire site.

Fonts should be easily readable in many styles (bold, italics, underlined) and consistent across the platform and in a standard size (10 or 12 point). Text size should be consistent throughout the platform, and easily readable on mobile devices and compatible with accessibility technologies, like text-to-speech services. This is another way that students access course materials, and that level of accessibility may be key to their success in the course (CAST, 2011). Course developers should avoid colorful or artistic fonts. Certain color combinations make some fonts difficult to read, especially on mobile devices and for the visually impaired (Harper, Michailidou, Stevens, 2009).

When implementing MMoR, it is possible to convey information in written form or with graphs, images, or other forms of media. If embedding pictures, it is important to provide an alt-text describing the image in detail, which allows students with visual impairments who have accessibility technology to interact with the materials. If there is video or audio utilized, then it should also have accurate captions and/or a full transcript included. This is helpful not only for students with impairments, but potentially useful for all learners, as some may be more partial to the visual learning that videos and pictures provide, while others might receive the benefit of reading the information via text or hearing it on a podcast.

Phraseology involves considering the composure of text on the course. The context should be generally understandable, while phrases and texts with multiple meanings or connotations should generally be avoided to achieve clarity. The language should be simple, clear, and concise. Developers must spend time developing and organizing content in a way that it is understandable, flows, and sensible. All of these elements also apply to the implementation of links. Links to external resources need spelling out with the complete universal resource locator (URL) and open in a separate tab or page within the user's browser.

Site Elements and Navigation

Furthermore, the site elements of the platform must also remain consistent throughout the website. Site elements include navigation, use of links, toolbars, and menus. As with the content and design, once again consideration for the UDL guidelines applies. It is essential that online learning environments be created utilizing the standards set forth by special education and online pedagogies, utilizing UDL as a guide. As suggested by online pedagogy, we recommend that classes to be broken down into microunits (smaller, weekly divisions of information) throughout the semester (McLoughlin and Lee, 2008). Communication is a key guideline in UDL and should be a constant feature in your learning environment. For example, peers express themselves and interact with the professors utilizing the discussion sections in every week. An announcements page keeps students informed of any new information, including changes and up-to-the-minute news items. Developing a scaffold of peers, professors, and experts not only supports effective delivery in the online community, allowing for peer-to-peer collaboration. Providing resources for the students, specific for each week and overarching for the whole course utilizing multiple modalities is essential to student learning and included in the learning environment.

Adherence to the UDL guidelines and standards will ensure the broadest level compatibility, regulatory compliance, platform usability, and information accessibility. One method that incorporates the best practices of online and special education pedagogies is the use of top-level navigation structure. Top-level navigation structure organizes content onto a single page accessible to users in one click (see **Figure 2**). This style gathers important information and presents it to users quickly without going through multiple webpages or levels of navigation, organizing the content in clear, concise, and accessible. Top-level navigation also promotes the use of mobile devices as information is easier to load and access on smartphones and mobile-Internet devices, allowing students multiple means of accessing the information based on their device.

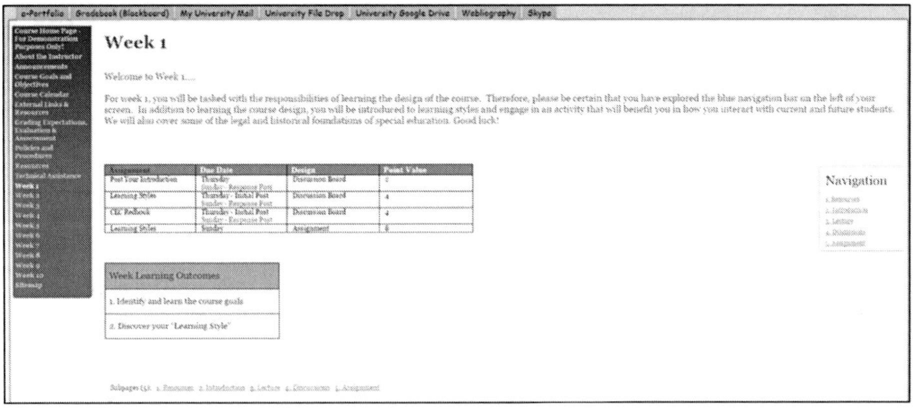

Figure 8.2: Example of Top-Level Navigation, Side-Level Navigation

In the navigation example above, each page is considered a "main-page"—a webpage devoted to important course-wide information. The information on main-pages is usually derived from a course syllabus, university/departmental policy, or other important sources. This is where the content of a site merges with the design. **Table 8.3** below specifies each course section from Figure 2, while briefly describing the content in each section.

Table 8.3: Online Course Sections and Content Delivery Methods

Course Section	Content
About the Instructor	The section introduces the instructor. This can include a brief biography, and also the contact information and office hours.
Announcements	This section provides up-to-the-minute updates regarding the course. Announcements are also emailed to all the students when the page updates.
Course Goals and Objectives	Lists not only the CEC standards, but the goals that each student are expected to meet throughout the semester.
Course Calendar	A week-by-week breakdown of the assignments, their due dates, and point values for the entire course.
External Links and Resources	Links for the online gradebook, e-mail, file drop, cloud storage, and webliography.
Grading Expectations, Evaluation, and Assessment	Detailed overviews of each assignment, how each are graded, and how the point values are distributed through the course.
Policies and Procedures	Policies and procedures as mandated by the university.
Resources	A listing of required texts, required articles, suggested texts, and suggested articles, with links and downloads when applicable.
Technical Assistance	Information regarding getting help from the staff technician regarding the online course. Also includes minimum system requirements to run the website.
Weeks 1–12	Where the lectures, discussions, and weekly learning outcomes are housed. Microunits vary in length depending on whether a 10-week or 12-week course.
Sitemap	Listing of all the above components of the course for ease of access.

This course is divided into multiple sections: About the instructor, announcements, course goals and objectives, course calendar, external links and resources, grading expectations/evaluation and assessment, policies and procedures, resources, technical assistance, weeks 1–12 (varying from course-to-course in length), and the sitemap. Each week is broken down into several subpages, which include: resources, lectures, discussions, assignment/test/quiz. Each section is accessible from every other page via a link. Each week has its own webpage, further subdivided into subpages. Subpage organization is developed according to the secondary navigation concept. Weekly subpages include resources, introduction, lecture, discussions, and assignment.

The introduction page is only used in week one. As the title would suggest, this page provides information which familiarizes students to the course and describes the course structure. Most platforms incorporate this element into the homepage. The website homepage is the starting point for instructors and students to access the course. Along with the introduction, students can access general information including a course calendar, instructor biography, contact information, and university/school policies and procedures. The lecture page includes the weekly lecture which may be provided in any of several formats—audio-only recordings, multimedia presentations, or videos that implement one or more programs like Microsoft PowerPoint, Google Hangout, YouTube video, or Apple Podcast. The discussions page provides a discussion topic for students to examine, and a place for students to deliberate and collaborate. There are multiple options when developing the discussion page, such as a Google Hangout, chat, forum, or shared blogpost; it is up to the course designers to determine which format works best for their online program. The final subpage is dedicated for assignments. The assignments page includes a summary of the assignment, links to additional resources surrounding the assignments, and a link to the specific platform where the assignment may be submitted.

Course overview and instruction is composed of the format and purpose of the course, and ensuring that it is clearly stated to each student at the start of the semester. Learning objectives and competencies must also be stated clearly for students and be measurable. Assessment strategies are architected to measure student progress in connection with the learning objectives, as well as evaluating the effectiveness of the program itself. Instructional materials can be composed of a multitude of media, be it course literature, lectures, handouts, and audio/video files; these must be adequate and compendious to achieve both learning outcomes and course objectives. Communication and interaction methods should promote accessibility, instruction, encourage collaboration, and motivate students to learn. Likewise, the course technology should reinforce student engagement through its format, technology supports, and navigation to assure access to course components. Student support is also critical, as the distance education program should promote access to institutional supports vital to student success. Finally, the platform and course design should illustrate an adherence to accessibility standards and policies for *ALL* students.

UDL Infusion with Course Design

Carrying over from the development of course content is the consideration and implementation of the UDL guidelines. UDL is an integral component of our online coursework design. It meets the needs of education and online pedagogies while allowing a way to present online coursework through flexible, accessible means (Scott, Temple, and Marshall, 2015). When discussing the general standards, we developed **Table 8.4** that not only lists each of the principles and guidelines of UDL but also provides examples of how each is delivered in online education.

Table 8.4: Online Course Design with UDL Checklist

I. Provide Multiple Means of Representation	1. Provide options for perception: • Options that customize the display of information. • Options that provide alternatives for auditory and visual information. *Example*: Video/audio and slide presentations that the professor shows and that the students develop include transcripts for diverse learners and reinforce UDL concepts.	2. Provide options for language and symbols: • Options that define the vocabulary and symbols. • Options that illustrate key concepts non-linguistically. *Example*: To introduce students to new technologies over the course of the semester, every assignment can be completed using a different type of tool (ex. Voki, vlogs, audio recordings) to narrate and explain graphical concepts.	3. Provide options for comprehension: • Options that highlight critical features, ideas, and relationships. • Options that support memory and transfer. *Example*: Instructors highlight key elements using text, graphics, and diagrams, while providing a brief checklist of core concepts on the side of the website via navigation bar.

Table 8.4: continued

II. Provide Multiple Means of Action and Expression	4. Provide options for physical action: • Options for accessing tools and assistive technologies. • Options in the means of navigation. • Options in the mode of physical responses. *Example*: Courses utilize Google Sites as a framework by which we provide information and literature that is accessible via multiple techno-logical and physical mediums (assigned textbooks, PDF files, and websites that can be accessed via traditional and tech-nological means.)	5. Provide options for expressive skills and fluency: • Options in media for communication. • Options in tools for composition and problem solving. • Options in the scaffolds for practice and performance. *Example*: Discus-sion assignments task students with the opportunity to choose what kind of presentation (PowerPoint, Voki, oral report, etc.) to demonstrate mastery of materials, share it within the discussion boards, and challenge other students with questions they have developed based on their understanding of the material.	6. Provide options for executive functions: • Options that guide goal-setting. • Options that support planning and strategy development. • Options that enhance capacity for monitoring progress. *Example*: In addition to the discussion boards, additional boards are set up for in-class groups to engage in discus-sions with each other regarding assignments, as well as a space for the entire class to get feedback from the professor and teach-ing assistant(s).

Table 8.4: continued

III. Provide Multiple Means of Engagement	7. Provide options for recruiting interest: • Options that increase individual choice, and autonomy. • Options that enhance relevance, value, and authenticity. *Example*: Students will write a case position paper regarding a court case on a topic (ex. LRE, evaluation, eligibility) that describes the facts, issues, and findings of the order; students themselves get to choose both the topic and a case that interests them.	8. Provide options for sustaining effort and persistence: • Options that vary levels of challenge and support. • Options that foster collaboration and communication. *Example*: Working together in groups of 2–3, students will develop a team teaching lesson plan for a grade 6–12 class utilizing UDL techniques. Students will also collaborate to create a brief visual presentation that also meet UDL standards.	9. Provide options for self-regulation: • Options to guide personal goal-setting and expectations. • Options that develop self-assessment and reflections. *Example*: Each site has a section devoted to grading expectations, evaluation, and assessment, where students can see the point values and determine the expectations of the course. Students are also encouraged to reflect on the materials via weekly discussions.

With these standards and guidelines in mind, program management, course developers, and instructors should begin by establishing goals for the course and considering how best to implement the guidelines of UDL. Instructors must consider what lessons, information, or skills are absorbed by the completion of the course, and the best ways to convey that information. UDL is not a catch-all; you may not utilize each guideline in your course. That said, instructors should strive to use multiple methods of instruction and learning to cater to an expanding scope of learning styles and technological advancement.

Starting with providing multiple means of representation, lectures are traditionally the key means of delivering information to students. The use of video and audio is used to replace the traditional classroom lecture, creating videos and podcasts or finding them when appropriate. This is enhanced by also including transcripts for non-visual learners, and incorporating exercises within the "lecture." You can also introduce students to new types of technologies that they can then use in their own classrooms. For example, you can use an introduction spoken by a virtual avatar using Voki, allowing students to experience a technology they may not have been familiar with before. As seen in Figure 2, a list of core concepts on the sidebar of every weekly page give students a way to stay focused on targeted lesson concepts, and these lesson targets are reinforced on the main page of every weekly lesson.

Providing multiple means of action and expression is the next row of UDL guidelines. Physical action may seem counterintuitive to an online environment, but even providing .PDF files of articles, transcripts, and assigning textbooks allows students to encounter the material digitally, listen to it via e-reader, or make print copies. Being able to express and show fluency of materials are key to the learning experience. As stated before, it is essential to introduce students to the types of technologies that they could use in their classrooms. Encourage students to utilize at least one new form of technology per assignment to show their mastery of the material and the medium. To ensure that a student's executive cognitive needs are being met, consider including safe areas for the students to discuss with each other and the instructors about concepts within the material.

Engagement is the final principle in UDL. Maintaining learner's interest is integral to the learning process, because if students are not engaged, then they will not begin to interpret or learn the information (CAST, 2011). Provide assignments that give students options in how they engage the material, such as allowing them to present on the findings of a scientific study of their own choosing that relates to the topic at hand. Provide options that allow students to learn collaborative skills and maintain a challenge; have students work together in small groups within and outside of the course. This grants them an opportunity to learn the collaborative skills that they will need to develop to be successful. Finally, providing options for self-regulation is critical to developing an engaged learner. Explicitly outline the grading expectations for the course as a whole within the syllabus, and reinforce these expectations within the weekly lessons by providing a list of that week's learning goals.

Accessibility and Accommodations Considerations

Digital inclusion and information accessibility are broad considerations when constructing an online instruction program. Accessibility, in some contexts, means the ability of people with a range of different types of abilities, including those with visual acuity, sound acuity, mobility, and symbolic processing challenges to access an online course and curriculum (Hai-Jew, 2010). In our design, however, accessibility is not limited to individuals with disabilities or other impairments. It is important to take into consideration the learning styles of our students. These may differ from person to person, from those who are visual in their learning, to those who prefer audio, or students who lean towards more traditional methods of learning. In broad terms, designing a course around accessibility ensures websites and platforms are easy to use for everyone, whether or not they have disabilities.

Other policy considerations would include ownership of intellectual property and student privacy rights. These will differ from institution to institution, and may incorporate such issues as public availability of materials, ownership of advertising rights on videos created for a course, or ensuring the security of students' contact and academic information. Federal law requires publicly accessible websites operated by federal and state agencies to comply with federal web accessibility standards. While private institutions may be exempted from these policies, others may face penalties for noncompliance. The Americans with Disabilities Act (ADA, 1990) is broad, and its legislation encompasses a variety of civil rights law that prohibits discrimination based on disability and certain federally protected classes. Specifically, the ADA addresses telecommunications with people with disabilities, including websites. According to the ADA, websites and certain Internet-enabled platforms must comply with accessibility standards for the blind, deaf, hard of hearing, and those with other disabilities (United States Department of Justice, 2010).

The Family Education Rights and Privacy Act of 1974 (FERPA), protects student non-directory information. Academic records including grades, health information, demographics and more are exempt from public disclosure unless the student or eligible parent/guardian consents otherwise. Students have a right to their own image and voice; therefore, instructors may consider having students sign legal agreements and consent forms at the beginning of the course to allow their use in recorded video and audio discussions (Hai-Jew, 2010). These agreements should specify how their information is used and obtained from them in the course. Legislation in many states may dictate what options are available in your school district or university. Federal and state legislation, in addition to any school district, university or department policies, may guide how websites should be constructed with accessibility in mind.

Stages 3 and 4—Course Review and Implementation

The review process may be divided into two parts: pre-enrollment review and post-enrollment review. Prior to implementation or enrollment, the online platform is reviewed by entities other than the course developer or technologist. The technologist observes a test user (an individual or small group of individuals who are not enrolled in the class) interacting with the site, and documents the results to ensure functionality as expected (Virginia Commonwealth University, 2013). The platform test user must have accesses to the entire platform, and should be granted the permissions necessary to fully navigate the course. The technologist observes the test user during this time, notating each error or issue that arises and corrects the issue. This pre-implementation review allows technical issues to be addressed and corrected before the students access the course. Once the instructors and the technologist have thoroughly tested the course, students are enrolled in the online environment and the class begins.

Orientation

Students should have access to or attend an online orientation session to familiarize themselves with the course features, such as the chatrooms, discussion forums, and interacting with documents and media files (Crawford-Ferre and Wiest, 2012). Once students have acclimated themselves with the course layout, the facilitation of learning happens much more quickly. Instructors may also find it useful to include a page with resources and frequently asked questions to assist users. Students are not the only ones who will need time to familiarize themselves with a new online format. Some instructors within your department will likely be new to the concept of online instruction. In addition to designing the online courses, the technologist and course developers must construct a parallel training program for instructors and students. Instructors need adequate training to improve competency, familiarity, and knowledgeability of the platform (Crawford-Ferre and Wiest, 2012). The technologist also ensures instructors have support and technical training beyond the online program. Online instruction requires all instructors have access to and training on the technology used in the program. Broad exposure to the technologies used in the program affords instructors a comfort which would otherwise be absent.

Instructors should also review the course in this process to ensure instructional needs have been satisfied. Course developers, program management and instructors must also devise a method to determine what students have learned. This method goes beyond general grading and assessment strategies; post-implementation review consists of assessing the usefulness of the platform and content. Program management investigates the best methods of receiving student feedback. Instructors should use formal and informal student feedback methods throughout the duration of the course. This feedback can be implemented to plan or alter instruction and assessment of student learning throughout the semester. For example, multimedia options such as online or mobile surveys gather critical information on the utility of the online platform and course. This is part of the post-enrollment review or feedback process. Maintaining consistent review protocols allows students to collaborate with instructors, which in turn allows instructors to develop and alter the course to better serve future students.

Conclusion

UDL is a set of principles and guidelines to allow the vast and varied learner base to learn and process new information. As stated before, your online course may not feature each guideline, as they may not be appropriate based on the course content. This should not dissuade you, however, from striving to implement multiple means of representation, action, and engagement in your online courses. Quite the opposite; this should be considered a challenge to deliver content in a better way for learners to gain the knowledge and skills that, as an instructor, you wish to impart on them. There is a fair amount of fluidity and creativity when designing an online course utilizing UDL. Online education is an ever-changing and amorphous concept, and can be intimidating when first approaching it. Using our conceptual framework, however, you can build an online learning environment that is every bit as innovative and informational as other learning institutions.

Implications for the Future

The overarching goal for this book was to present ideas for consideration when designing online courses, highlighting strategies used by experts for designing online courses for distance education programs. The authors sought to gather details about UDL and online pedagogy that would be relevant to identify standards or guidelines for online instruction and online course design. As we showcased in our model, UDL may offer ways to enhance the design and delivery of an online course. The UDL framework in a distance education course or program can offer that specialized design that we sought and can positively impact learning and preparation (Scott, Temple, Marshall, 2015). But while the design of a course that follows a UDL framework is promising, additional exploration is necessary to gain more insight about UDL and implications for distance education courses and programs. We believe it's important the field continues to engage in this conversation and that research studies be designed to test hypotheses and refine our practices.

For example, there remain concerns over whether online learning can truly prepare highly effective and qualified teachers. Those who challenge the efficacy of online teacher preparation perceive online coursework as less rigorous when compared to face-to-face preparation (Columbaro and Monaghan, 2009); pedagogy associated with online instruction as second-rate (Cox, 2005); and limited face-to-face interaction between instructor and student which they argue leads to poor preparation and low online course completion (Bambara, Harbour, Davies, and Athey, 2009). We question whether those concerns reflect more on the quality of the strategies used for online courses rather than online programs as a whole. For distance education programs, it is critically important that we get the online course design and delivery correct so that preparation standards are not lowered.

There are also certain conclusions that we draw from our research and experience. First, we are confident that a UDL framework can assist in merging content and online pedagogy for the design and delivery of online courses. Second, we are confident in the ability to embed UDL principles and are confident that using this framework, others who use this approach will be able to effectively prepare and bring positive changes to their distance education courses and programs. We know that the list of ways to embed UDL principles with content and pedagogy is not exhausted in this book. We also recognize that the UDL principles and guidelines presented are extensive and can be overwhelming for planning and designing. However, our goal was to provide and share this model as a starting point for faculty, post-secondary institutions that are interested in specialized online design and delivery, and other stakeholders. We also strongly believe that this design and delivery can make positive impacts for students' enrolled in distance education courses and programs. We are encouraged that those who choose to apply the framework will have similar experiences, and we welcome an opportunity to engage in next steps with all of you.

References

Becker, S., Coward, C., Crandall, M., Sears, R., Carlee, R., Hasbargen, K., and Ball, M. A. (2012). *Building Digital Communities: A Framework for Action.* Washington, DC: Institute of Museum and Library Services.

Blackboard [Computer Software] (2016). Retrieved from http://blog.blackboard.com/.

Center for Applied Special Technology, (2008). *Universal Design for Learning Guidelines,* version 1.0. Retrieved from www.udlcenter.org/sites/udlcenter.org/files/GPS_article_final_2.doc.

Center for Applied Special Technology, (2011). *Universal Design for Learning Guidelines,* version 2.0. Wakefield, MA: Author.

Crawford-Ferre, H. G., and Wiest, L. R. (2012). "Effective Online Instruction in Higher Education." *The Quarterly Review of Distance Education,* 13(1), 11–14.

Dey, A. K., Abowd, G. D., and Salber, D. (2000). "A context-based infrastructure for smart environments." In *Managing Interactions in Smart Environments* (pp. 114–128). Springer London.

Edmodo [Computer Software] (2016). Retrieved from https://www.edmodo.com/.

Google (2016). Google Apps for Education [Computer Program]. Retrieved from https://www.google.com/edu/products/productivity-tools/.

Hai-Jew, S. (2010, December 15). "An Instructional Design Approach to Updating an Online Course Curriculum." *Educase Review.* Retrieved from http://er.educause.edu/articles/2010/12/an-instructional-design-approach-to-updating-an-online-course-curriculum#ART.

Harper, S., Michailidou, E., and Stevens, R. (2009). "Toward a definition of visual complexity as an implicit measure of cognitive load." *ACM Transactions on Applied Perception (TAP),* 6(2), 10.

Livingstone, S., and Helsper, E. (2007). Gradations in digital inclusion: Children, young people and the digital divide. *New media & society,* 9(4), 671–696.

Murray, T. (1998). "Authoring knowledge-based tutors: Tools for content, instructional strategy, student model, and interface design." *The Journal of the Learning Sciences,* 7(1), 5–64.

Page, C. (2015, August 25). *Accessible Information Technology.* Retrieved from South Carolina Assistive Technology Program: https://www.sc.edu/scatp/ITaccessibility.htm.

Quality Matters. (2014). *Higher Ed Program>Rubric|Quality Matters.* Retrieved November 16, 2015, from https://www.qualitymatters.org/rubric.

Teo, H. H., Chan, H. C., Wei, K. K., and Zhang, Z. (2003). "Evaluating information accessibility and community adaptivity features for sustaining virtual learning communities." *International Journal of Human-Computer Studies*, 59(5), 671–697.

United States Department of Justice. (2010, September 15). *2010 ADA Standards for Accessible Design*. Retrieved from Information and Technical Assistance on the Americans with Disabilities Act: http://www.ada.gov/2010ADAstandards_index.htm.

Virginia Commonwealth University. (2013, September 16). *Best Practices VCU Web Standards & Guidelines*. Retrieved from VCU Web Standards & Guidelines: http://www.webstandards.vcu.edu/best/.

Watson, W. R., and Watson, S. L. (2007). "What are learning management systems, what are they not, and what should they become?" *TechTrends*, 51(2), 29.

Wordpress [Computer Program] (2016). Retrieved from https://wordpress.com/.